THE WASHINGTON PAPERS
Volume VIII

74: German-American Relations

W. R. Smyser

Preface by Richard Lowenthal

THE CENTER FOR STRATEGIC AND INTERNATIONAL STUDIES
Georgetown University, Washington, D.C.

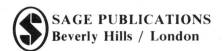
SAGE PUBLICATIONS
Beverly Hills / London

327.73
S667g

For information address:

SAGE PUBLICATIONS, INC.
275 South Beverly Drive
Beverly Hills, California 90212

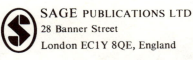

SAGE PUBLICATIONS LTD
28 Banner Street
London EC1Y 8QE, England

International Standard Book Number 0-8039-1451-2

Library of Congress Catalog Card No. 79-57535

FIRST PRINTING

When citing a Washington Paper, please use the proper form. Remember to cite the
series title and include the paper number. One of the two following formats can be
adapted (depending on the style manual used):

(1) HASSNER, P. (1973) "Europe in the Age of Negotiation." The Washington
Papers, I, 8. Beverly Hills and London: Sage Pubns.

OR

(2) Hassner, Pierre. 1973. *Europe in the Age of Negotiation.* The Washington Papers,
vol. 1, no. 8. Beverly Hills and London: Sage Publications.

81-1498

C O N T E N T S

FOREWORD

German-American relations constitute a vital concern to the entire international community and represent a particularly important subject for American policymakers at this time. We are, therefore, pleased to present in this Washington Paper a study on German-American relations by a Fellow at the Georgetown University Center for Strategic and International Studies, Dr. W. R. Smyser. His academic background and diplomatic experience enable him to deal thoroughly, yet succinctly, with vital issues basic to this relationship.

We are also pleased to present a preface by Professor Richard Lowenthal, a member of our Center's Research Council. The points raised by Professor Lowenthal underline both the importance of German-American relations and some of the different perceptions held by scholars in both countries.

David M. Abshire
Chairman, CSIS
February, 1980

PREFACE

At a difficult juncture in international affairs, when the
United States is counting its real friends in the world, it is
natural that it should reexamine its relations with the Federal
Republic of Germany. Born more than 30 years ago from the
ruins of defeat and nursed with American protection and
substantial aid for its reconstruction, that country has developed into one of the most important and stable allies of the
United States. In the same process, however, what was once
little more than a protectorate has become a medium-sized
power in its own right, showing great economic and considerable military strength and also growing independence in the
pursuit of its national interests, thanks to the increased
freedom of diplomatic movement acquired by its *Ostpolitik*.
Though Western Germany is conscious of its dependence on
American nuclear protection as well as of the network of
common interests and outlook tying it to the Western alliance, its rise from the status of a client state to that of a full
partner inevitably raises a number of problems. It is the
purpose of Dr. Smyser's paper to make his readers conscious
of those problems, not in a spirit of distrust, but, on the
contrary, in order to show that they can be solved in a spirit
of goodwill on both sides, and thus to strengthen the basis
for long-term cooperation.

Dr. Smyser is well qualified for that important task, both
by his keen analytic mind and by his diplomatic experience.
His ten years of diplomatic service in Germany have made
him a friend of the Federal Republic, but, fortunately, not an

uncritical friend. Looking myself at the problems of German-American relations from the German point of view, I find that Dr. Smyser has dealt with them with fairness, objectivity, and a great deal of discernment. His paper, in my view, constitutes an important contribution to the future cooperation between both countries.

I may be permitted, however, to add three remarks of my own to the content of the paper; two are in the nature of additions, while one is more of a criticism. My first remark refers to the causes of the development of a new type of relationship between the United States and the Federal Republic—what Dr. Smyser calls their "equivalence." It seems to me important to realize that this is due not only to a growth of German strength and freedom of movement, but also to a certain reduction in the world role of the United States, a reduction that Germans observe with misgivings. In part, that reduction is the inevitable consequence of the changing structure of international relations, the rise of new powers, the new problems of assuring the supply of energy and raw materials for the industrial countries; in part, however, it appears to be due to internal causes that have at least temporarily diminished the domestic American consensus on foreign policy, hence American capacity for international action, including in some cases international negotiation. This state of affairs may be overcome, since it is not due to an objective reduction of the resources available to American foreign policy. But while it lasts, it is important in our context, because it raises questions about the stability and consistency of that policy in Germany: anxiety about the alliance does not exist on one side only.

My second remark concerns Dr. Smyser's view of the future of the international environment. Because he thinks it unlikely that East-West negotiations will in the future be as fruitful of major results as in the early years of detente, he foresees a long period where conflicts will be more acute than in those years though different than at the height of the Cold

War. To my mind, the crucial question at the present time is not whether East-West negotiations will be very fruitful but whether a constructive negotiating relationship can be maintained at all, particularly in the field of nuclear armaments, because with the present relation of world forces such a relationship seems to me vital for avoiding the risk of nuclear war. The Germans, owing to the benefits they derived from detente, may be especially aware of this need; but its urgency is not based on particular German or European interests, but on the interest of the survival of mankind.

My critical remark concerns the contrast drawn by Dr. Smyser between the historic and intellectual backgrounds of American and West German economic policy, attributing to the former a basically "Keynesian" concern with full employment and to the latter a basically "monetarist" bias due to the historic trauma of two German inflations. I believe that Dr. Smyser not only overestimates the stability of the Keynesian commitment in the United States—the Eisenhower recession was certainly due to a non-Keynesian policy, and at present the pressure of "monetarist" tendencies seems again very strong to me—but above all that he underestimates the Keynesian element in West German economic policy ever since the Social Democrats first entered the Federal Government at the end of 1966. The "stability law" passed by the Grand Coalition in 1967 is based on strict Keynesian doctrine, and Helmut Schmidt, the present Chancellor, is on record as saying that he should rather have a five percent inflation than five percent unemployment; in fact, he has succeeded in keeping not only the rate of inflation but *also* the rate of unemployment lower than other major western countries including the United States. I believe that Dr. Smyser may have been overly impressed by the differences between American and German economic policies during the first two years of the Carter administration; but they were based, in my opinion, not on different economic doctrines but on different estimates of the concrete situation—and they disappeared when the German estimate had proved to be more correct in that case.

Dr. Smyser shrewdly observes that close cooperation with Germany on a basis of "equivalence" has no long tradition in American policy, as has similar cooperation with Britain or France: the habit has to be acquired, and acquired by a new generation of political, economic, and cultural elites that was not "present at the creation" of the alliance. He shows the points where differences may arise in the fields of world politics, of relations with the East or the Third World, in economics, and in the field of security, and he gives convincing reasons why the common interests are strong and stable enough to overcome all those differences, if a careful and responsible effort is made on both sides. His plea is for a "consistent stewardship" to ensure that effort. It is with a profound conviction founded on the experience of the entire postwar era that I join this plea.

Richard Lowenthal
Fellow, National Humanities Center
North Carolina

AUTHOR'S PREFACE

R elations between the United States and the Federal
Republic of Germany have become an issue of vital
concern. As the Federal Republic has become more influential in world affairs, its relationship with America needs a
closer look. The purpose of this paper is to examine that
relationship, its background, and its future prospects.

This paper does not catalogue all current or potential
issues in the current German-American relationship. That
would take too long, since it would include virtually all
significant international problems. Nor does the paper describe personal relations of senior officials. Those relations can
change. Instead, it looks at the foundations of the relationship and uses some central topics to illustrate its importance
and its complexity.

Such a study must concentrate on differences in order to
explain them, but not to glorify them. In German-American
relations, common interests far outweigh differences. This
said, the precise nature of the differences must be understood.

I frequently use the term "Germany" or "Germans" to
mean the government and the people of the Federal Republic
of Germany. This is not intended to ignore the existence of
the German Democratic Republic, but for the sake of brevity. Nor should it conceal that in Germany, as in any democratic society, differences of opinion exist within the country. For the most part, such differences do not affect German-American affairs, but will be cited where they do.

I am a Foreign Service Officer. I have written this work while at the Georgetown University Center for Strategic and International Studies as a Foreign Affairs Fellow. The work represents my own views and not those of the United States government or any of its agencies.

To write the paper, I have drawn on my own knowledge as well as on a number of written sources listed at the end as "References." Readers who want to study in more detail any of the particular subjects dealt with in the paper may wish to look at those references.

German-American relations cover such a wide area that no-one can master all aspects fully. Therefore, I have presumed upon some knowledgeable friends and colleagues to read the manuscript, either in whole or in part, and to offer suggestions for its improvement. I am deeply grateful for this help; I, of course, accept responsibility for shortcomings. Those who read the manuscript, in Germany and in the United States, did so in their private capacity and are, therefore, not identified by organization or title: Fred Bergsten, Thomas Callaghan, William Cates, Benjamin Cohen, Wayne Cole, Peter Corterier, Wolfgang Engels, Guenther Gillessen, Guido Goldman, Michael Habib, Robert Hormats, Hans-Adolf Jacobsen, Karl Kaiser, Philip Kaplan, Manfred Knapp, Lawrence Krause, Richard Lowenthal, Edward Luttwak, John Mapother, Klaus Mehnert, Kenneth Myers, Uwe Nerlich, Klaus Ritter, Sterling Slappey, Marten Van Heuven, John Yochelson, and David Willey.

I would like also to express my deep appreciation to Evelyn Burns for her patient and effective assistance in the preparation of the manuscript.

W. R. Smyser
Washington, D.C.

I. EQUIVALENCE

German-American relations face a difficult new task: the management of equivalence. This German-American equivalence is unspoken, unacknowledged, often denied, and perhaps even unwanted. Yet, it is a central reality for both countries.

Equivalence in this sense must be carefully defined. The United States and the Federal Republic are not equal in all forms of power. The power balance between them is highly asymmetrical. Yet, they are equivalent in a most fundamental way: both constitute essential pillars of an international system which they wish to preserve. Neither can successfully preserve that system without the other, while either could do serious damage to basic interests, including the safety and well-being, of the other.

The Federal Republic and the United States are not equal in military terms. The United States possesses the world's largest arsenal of nuclear weapons. U.S. security guarantees remain essential to the safety of the Federal Republic, as of any other states. Germans do not want nuclear weapons and would not be able to obtain them without creating serious political repercussions. German military strength lies in conventional weapons and forces. German armed forces defend the largest portions of the crucial East-West boundary that runs through the center of what used to be the German Empire and that must, therefore, in the first instance be defended on German soil.

In economics, the balance is closer if also asymmetrical. The German economy is smaller than that of the United States. However, Germany now holds the world's largest monetary reserves. It has higher productivity than the United States. The German D-Mark has for some years been stronger than the U.S. dollar and has become a world currency. Germany plays a central role in the creation and functioning of a new European monetary system. Frankfurt has again become what it was in the past: one of the financial and trading centers of the world.

Germany, like the United States, plays a key role in international political matters. During a stretch of four months in 1978, the Chairman of the Soviet Communist Party, the Queen of England, the President of the United States, and the Vice Premier of China visited Bonn. The Federal Republic conducts relations with more than 140 different countries and its support is sought by every significant capital. It has gained wide-spread international respect. German policies toward the Soviet Union and Eastern Europe, known under the broad heading of *Ostpolitik*, constitute an essential and recognized element of a stable international system. Germany is one of the Summit powers of the West.

It is simply anachronistic to utter the old phrases that "Germany is an economic giant but a political dwarf," or that "the Germans are on their way to becoming an influential nation." The Germans have arrived.

An element of irony pervades Germany's rise to power and influence. Under its emperors and Hitler, Germany sought world power for many years. It did reach, but soon lost, such power. Now, Germany does not seek world power. It attempts consistently to camouflage its own capacity to act. It insists on a low profile, on an image smaller than reality. Nonetheless, the new Germany has gained greater international eminence and respect than those German governments that conspicuously reached for them.

German power and influence have not changed the country's fundamental interests, which broadly parallel America's. Like the United States, Germany wants and needs peace as well as world-wide political and military stability. It wants an international system in which free governments can act freely and can jointly defend themselves. It wants a liberal international economic environment. It wants a strong Atlantic alliance as well as a strong and prosperous Western Europe.

If German interests have not changed, what has changed is Germany's ability to preserve and protect those interests. For decades, the Federal Republic relied upon the United States to provide security and to maintain international political, economic, and financial stability. Today, Germans can do much more to protect and preserve their own interests. Their power and influence will probably continue to grow. They can and do act on their own, not on the basis of American suggestion, although usually in concert with the United States and with other members of the Atlantic and European communities. The Germans often influence American views.

One might even term German-American relations one of interdependent equivalence. There are many points—to be discussed in subsequent chapters—at which the two states now rely on each other, often almost taking for granted that the other will help. Whether on international monetary problems, world political crises, or the development of modernized NATO nuclear systems, they cooperate closely, trying hard to settle problems as they arise. They do not always succeed, but neither could do as much separately as they can do together. They do not always agree, but often enough to sustain a close and still promising association.

A New International Environment

A new international environment, emerging ever more clearly over the past few years, has contributed to Germany's rise to power and influence. That environment has also spawned intricate dilemmas for German-American relations.

The new environment represents the third phase of international relations since the end of World War II.

—The first phase, the Cold War, saw Russian-American polarization lasting from the late 1940s through much of the 1960s. Confrontation then dominated relations between the two major powers. Even during that period of confrontation, there were efforts at relaxation of tension between the Soviet Union and the United States, but they did not succeed.

—The second phase, known as detente, brought partial settlement of certain issues between the Soviet Union and Western powers. It eased East-West tensions. During that phase, negotiations were as dominant as confrontations had been during the first phase. The second phase did not last very long because, as the word detente suggests, it was a time of relaxation of tension, a period of movement and transition, not a fixed state of affairs. Its purpose had been to terminate the abnormal world situation resulting from World War II.

—The third period, in which we now are, includes elements both of confrontation and negotiation. It can have crises as tense as those of the Cold War. On the other hand, the kind of diplomacy that dominated detente has not ceased altogether. The most important feature of this new era for policymakers is its inherent ambiguity. The new era may last for quite some time, perhaps longer than the Cold War and detente eras combined. Unlike Cold War Soviet-American confrontations, which resulted from disputes over the settlement of World War II, post-detente crises reflect a wider power conflict of global and potentially enduring dimensions.

This new era marks the return to a more traditional international environment. It is, of course, peculiar to this century. On the whole, however, the current era more closely resembles the traditional world environment of tension alleviated by diplomacy than did either the Cold War or detente.

Yet the word "traditional" does not properly reflect the extraordinary potential for instability within the present world order. Most of that instability originates outside the Western system, in adventurous Soviet policies in troubles of the Middle East and Africa, in uncertainties about successor governments in Moscow and other East European capitals, in escalating resource demands against limited and politically controllable supplies, in an increasingly perplexing international economic environment, and in the growing risk of nuclear proliferation. The greatest source of potential instability, perhaps, is the risk of miscalculation. The Cold War over time developed certain unwritten rules of behavior. In detente, new rules were presumed to prevail and some attempts were made to codify them. No rules yet exist for the post-detente era. Developing and testing them may be highly dangerous and also disruptive to Atlantic unity. All these instabilities can affect the West, including America and Germany, profoundly.

Diffusion of power is endemic to the new world system. In past centuries, Europe and its offspring states dominated the world, reinforcing even as they were battling each other, until the climactic European civil wars annihilated the old world order. Outside countries and events impact on Europe, the Soviet Union, and America, adding to uncertainty and frustration. Now, ancient conflicts suppressed by the European world order can surface again, perhaps drawing in different Atlantic powers even if those powers can no longer determine the outcome. The nations of the West, cohesive in the Cold War and detente, may not be able to remain together in dealing with these problems and tensions.

Despite this, the international system contains numerous opportunities for Western countries to exercise influence and power in various forms and to varying degrees, within and outside Europe, alone or together. Whereas, during the Cold War, diplomacy often appeared to be useless and became simply declamatory, and whereas, during detente, defense

expenditures appeared to be perfunctory and even provoca-
tive, in the new era diplomacy and arms have separate and
yet mutually supporting roles to play. So does economic
strength. In dealing with the Third World, economic power
and the capacity to manage a nation's destiny may count for
more than other traditionally respected forms of influence.
All countries have to find a combination that will be effective
abroad and accepted at home.

Detente departed in one very significant way from the
Cold War by allowing Germany a more prominent and important place. The Cold War had been marked by the over-
whelming power and influence of the United States and the
Soviet Union. Germany, still numb from World War II, phy-
sically and psychologically, had firmly allied itself with the
West and moved largely in tandem with the United States.
During detente, however, Germany began to come into its
own. Detente marked the return of Germany as a significant
actor in world affairs.

A further distinction also exists between the detente and
post-detente eras. Detente was marked by new departures,
new breakthroughs, new ideas, almost every month. A sense
of momentum dominated international politics. With old
rigidities disappearing, many believed—or hoped—that perhaps a new international order could be constructed. In the
cold light of the post-detente era, intractabilities become
more obvious. The result is a bleak perception that the future
will demand a difficult combination of determination and
patience. All interactions become more ambiguous, whether
between or within alliance systems. All Western relations
become, to some degree, trilateral, with the Soviet Union, the
Warsaw Pact, or some other state or group of states, an actual
or potential operative factor. The era of negotiations did not
bring lasting peace or systemic cooperation. It was not a new
beginning, only a new phase.

The crises in Iran and Afghanistan, beginning in 1979,
mirrored these dilemmas. The United States and other West-

ern nations wanted to react to violations of international law and stability. Yet they wished to move the world away from, not toward, war and illegality. Thus, they had to examine what aspects of their international relationships, including detente relationships, they still could and should try to preserve even as they confronted new and potentially explosive situations. They also had to act against the backdrop of growing dependence on the energy resources of the Persian Gulf, and in the face of considerable uncertainty about how access to those resources could best be secured.

The new world also brings deepening interdependence. The states of the West need each other as much if not more than ever. Even during confrontations with Moscow, they have certain common or separate links with the East, and those links have value for both partners. World-wide interdependencies exist, with China, Japan, and other states of Asia, with the Third World, and with the OPEC states. This interdependent world sometimes offers greater opportunities for maneuver than did the Cold War, but it also offers less room for new departures than did detente. More international business needs to be done to insure security in its new dimension—a dimension that is not just military—but no lasting solutions are available. The environment is perplexing as well as dangerous.

The West does not pass into that new era with each state isolated and at bay. Because of the close collaboration in detente, not only between Bonn and Washington but within the Western alliance system as a whole, that alliance system remained intact during the detente era although it had originally been conceived and constructed for the Cold War. The alliance system remains pervasive and influential to a degree that is difficult to understand for non-participants in its consultative and operational framework. The NATO Treaty and the Treaty of Rome have spawned living organisms with myriad contacts, channels, and opportunities for collaboration. An almost infinite variety of different issues, including many German-American questions, are handled and resolved within the structure of that alliance system.

America and Germany in the New World

The new international environment promotes German possibilities for influence. It requires states to pursue the combination of political and economic policies for which Germany's strength is well suited. Germany can use its growing political influence and economic resources in East and West, as well as in the Third World, to help protect its security interests. It can, by working with its partners in a European system in which it plays an increasingly important role, count not only on its own resources but often on those of Western Europe as a whole. More than before, Germany can try to find solutions by itself or with others than America.

The Federal Republic, however, also suffers from deep vulnerabilities. In dealing with Western nations, it must live with its history. In dealing with Eastern Europe and the Soviet Union, it must live with that history, with relative military weakness, and with the division of the German nation. In dealing with the Third World, and especially the resource countries, it must overcome its import dependence though history is no burden and even an advantage. It is, therefore, singularly exposed even as it is strong and influential. In security matters, in particular, Germany's options remain limited.

American vulnerabilities are increasing. It now depends on many foreign resources, most notably oil. American well-being is more exposed to outside events than before, whether those events are political or economic in nature. The United States can no longer chart its own course without concern for how others might react. It has to count on its allies more than before.

Although fundamentally stronger than Germany, America has not been able to bring its full strength to bear in the new international environment. Americans remain diffident, after the Vietnam and Watergate experiences, even about themselves, although events in Iran and Afghanistan sparked a rebirth of patriotic sentiment. Germans, in spite of their history and their objective vulnerabilities, sense that they are moving forward again. This gives them confidence. Americans, in spite of their strength and the demonstrated effectiveness of their system, sense that events are moving against them. Much of the relative decline in American power since the early postwar days represents nothing more than the re-establishment of a traditional international system in which no state can be fully dominant. Some of America's problems are temporary. Although Germany is more vulnerable than America, during the last few years America has been more often wounded, at the cost of confidence and some capacity to act.

The Federal Republic's position in Europe conditions many German attitudes and also plays a role in German-American relations. Often, German-American issues are European-American issues, with the Germans representing, or at least reflecting, the view of Western European states. On many disputes between Bonn and Washington, like human rights in Eastern Europe or the threat of nuclear proliferation through international nuclear power sales, other European states openly or tacitly support the Germans and often take even stronger positions. These issues reflect a growing European political consciousness. However, many of the difficulties that may arise are also contained and resolved within the Western alliance system itself. German power and influence have grown because the Federal Republic, unlike the German Empire, uses its strength in concert with other European states instead of against them.

The combination of greater German influence and the more difficult international climate makes differences of opinion between Germany and America more likely, and even magnifies them. In the past, Germany's role was not central to the solution of international difficulties. Now, the United States and Germany must coordinate on virtually all problems that may arise all over the globe, whether political, economic, or even military. The wide range of issues that require discussion makes disagreements more likely, and the ambiguous climate makes them certain.

The United States and the Federal Republic have had their differences in the postwar years, particularly in the 1960s, on a broad range of issues. But the issues now arising, and the differences of view, represent potentially greater problems. Then, it was commonly assumed in Bonn and Washington that all questions ultimately had to be resolved in Washington's favor because the Germans had few options. A German political leader could justify his decision to agree with the United States on the basis of pure and absolute necessity. Today, there is a sense that the Federal Republic has wider options, or that at the very least Germany must go along with *alliance* decisions, not with American wishes. Therefore, differences must be resolved on the basis of common agreement on the problem and on the policies necessary to solve it. Moreover, the range of issues on which differences can arise is wider than ever, and the cumulative effect can add to the tensions associated with each.

These problems impact on the psychology of the relationship. That psychology has constituted an important backdrop to relations since 1945. For Germany and the United States, 1945 represented a new beginning. Germany arose from ruins. The United States shed isolationism and moved bravely, if not without some reservations, into a new international role. Both countries started something new together. For each, the relationship with the other was the expression of this new start. For each, some initial common stands—whether at Berlin or elsewhere—represented the beginning of a new and significant relationship.

The Cold War deepened these attitudes. Without that Cold War, Americans would not as quickly have changed their views of the Germans. Without it, Germans would not have made some difficult choices that they had to make. During the Cold War, the United States and Germany more often followed policies in common with each other than they did with other allies. They welcomed each other's support, and they provided each other with vital complementarity in their security arrangements.

The German-American postwar relationship of unequal partners produced certain direct gratifications: for one partner, deep gratitude and a sense of being accepted back into the international community; for the other, the satisfaction of helping an errant fellow-nation find its way back. These gratifications are now things of the past. The Federal Republic is no longer a dependent. Instead, it is a pillar of the Western community. The new relationship is of companionable, close association, of collaboration as equals in the pursuit of common interests jointly perceived and agreed.

It is the perception of a common relationship as equals which raises the fundamental historical problem of the German-American relationship. Germany and the United States have never had a long and successful period of close association as equals. In this sense, German-American relations are very different from those between the Americans and the British or the French.

The times when German-American relations have been best, though not fully free of troubles and differences, have been the periods immediately after World Wars I and II, when the United States was dominant and Germany was weak. During most of the eighteenth and nineteenth centuries, even as streams of immigrants came from Germany to the United States, official relations remained at a cordial but distant level. Toward the end of the nineteenth century and in the early years of the twentieth century, as Germany and the United States were both rising to world power, a number of differences between the two countries emerged. They became rivals even before World War I. During the Hitler era, when both countries again were equals in power, even deeper differences arose and ultimately helped lead to war.

This lack of historical association contributes a brittle quality to the German-American relationship. It has less sense of resiliency, less automatic assurance that, no matter how serious any disagreement may be, that disagreement will be overcome and things set to rights. The cooperative tradition, if there is to be one, must be established now, under all the pressures and tensions of the present world.

With the United States and the Federal Republic representing equally vital, although not twin, pillars of the international and Western systems, the German-American relationship becomes more difficult just as it becomes more important. In fact, it becomes more difficult *because* it is more important. Yet the common interests shared by the two countries are so central to their existence that they cannot afford not to collaborate. Neither country can achieve any significant objective, political, economic, or strategic, without the support of the other. Leaders in Bonn and Washington deal with this reality every day. What they need to find is how to suit specific policies to the new realities so that the German-American relationship remains, for both countries, a source of strength.

II. POLITICAL RELATIONS

Nearly 60 years ago, in April, 1922, a major international gathering took place at Genoa, Italy, to seek ways of overcoming the deepening economic dislocations caused by World War I. It met in the shadow of the reparations assessment of 132 billion gold marks that had been levied on the infant German Republic. Organizers of the conference had gone so far as to invite the two pariahs, Germany and the Soviet Union, although those representatives found themselves largely isolated at Genoa. The conference failed to find a solution to international economic problems but it did provide the backdrop for a diplomatic bombshell.

On Easter morning, April 16, the Soviet and German delegations met at one of the lovely resort towns on the Ligurian Coast, Rapallo. There they signed an agreement, negotiated in the main before the Genoa Conference, waiving mutual claims and promising to improve relations. The treaty created the foundation for Soviet-German economic as well as secret military collaboration, which were to continue intermittently under Hitler and Stalin. It generated a major shock in the West, contributed to a French decision in 1923 to occupy the Ruhr industrial heart of Germany, and remains to this day the inspiration for the "Rapallo Complex"—the notion that Germany and Russia may yet reach another agreement that will turn Germany away from the West.

The significance of Rapallo, and its absolute irrelevance to current developments, lay not in the agreement between the Soviet Union and Germany. It lay in the absence of any

German anchor toward the West. In 1922, Germany was internationally isolated, humiliated, and friendless. At home, the new Republic was politically confused and unstable. It had literally nothing to lose. Today, the Federal Republic has firm ties to the West as well as a widening international role and a stable domestic environment.

In the past dozen years, Germany and the Soviet Union have signed a series of agreements. Those agreements deal with political and economic matters of considerable significance. If Germany had not been an ally of the United States and solidly anchored in the West, those agreements with the Soviet Union might already have been regarded as the equivalent of the Rapallo Agreement. That they were not so regarded is testimony to the circumstances under which they were negotiated and signed. The role of the United States has been central, although not unique, in creating those new and different circumstances.

This chapter will examine the relationship between German and American dealings with the Soviet Union. It will then examine German ties to the West in the context of German-American relations.

Relations with the East

After World War II, because of the victors' inability to agree on a policy or a peace treaty for all of Germany, the Western occupation zones of Germany were tied to the United States and the nations of Western Europe. The Federal Republic of Germany became a part of the West and, after the Berlin crisis and the Korean war, chose to accept a role in its defense. This policy of the government of Konrad Adenauer was supported by the West German populace in a series of crucial elections. Germany was divided. Borders between East and West Germany became sealed. The only remaining open border for some years was the sector/sector boundary in Berlin. The Wall sealed it in 1961, dividing Germany and Europe.

From the early 1960s, after the Berlin and Cuban crises, West Germany and the United States intensified efforts to improve relations with the Soviet Union and Eastern Europe. These efforts, in combination with Soviet policies, culminated in the late 1960s and early 1970s in the detente period of diplomacy. In a short stretch of several years, the Federal Republic negotiated agreements with the Soviet Union, Poland, and the German Democratic Republic (GDR). Those agreements essentially accepted the status quo for both sides. The United States, Britain, and France, in close consultation with the Federal Republic, negotiated the Berlin Quadripartite Agreement with Moscow, stabilizing the situation of the city and its access to and from the West. The United States also negotiated a series of bilateral accords, including SALT I, with the Soviet Union.

The distinction between German and American detente settlements with the Soviet Union lay in a crucial area. German negotiations with Moscow dealt with the original political core of the Cold War, whereas American negotiations dealt with the strategic core of the Cold War. Germany reached detente by negotiating with the East not on security matters, but on political reconciliation, borders, trade, and credits. The United States reached detente by negotiating primarily on crucial elements of the strategic balance. Germany did not need to negotiate security matters with the Soviet Union, since German security was guaranteed by the United States and by NATO. The only German role in security negotiations with Moscow has been in the Mutual and Balanced Force Reductions (MBFR) talks.

Although the United States and the Federal Republic negotiated with the Soviet Union on differing subjects, their policies reinforced each other. Just as they collaborated during the Cold War, Washington and Bonn collaborated during detente. If this had not been the case, it is doubtful whether either could have reached the objective of a new relationship with the East. The United States would have been hard put to negotiate a strategic settlement with the Soviet Union in the face of a crisis in, or tension around, Germany. Bonn would have found it impossible to negotiate a settlement with the Soviet Union if the United States had been engaged in a series of confrontations with the Soviet Union. Detente policy during the late 1960s and early 1970s remains an example of how the United States and Germany can, by separate though coordinated efforts, support each other in the attainment of common objectives.

Germany and the United States moved on approximately similar schedules toward detente, even in the early period of 1963-1965, and more when detente later flowered. At times, the United States was moving faster. At other times, Germany was. At times, some suspicion prevailed between them. On the whole, however, despite some differences in phasing and despite suspicion, they proceeded in parallel directions at roughly the same pace. Germany played a particular role, characterized by independent initiatives. Although most negotiations relating to central Europe were closely linked, whether they dealt with arms control, the Conference on Security and Cooperation in Europe (CSCE), Berlin, or East-West relations, Bonn negotiated on its own several agreements with the Soviet Union and other East European states. The Germans took diplomatic and political initiatives; they found formulas for accord; they also significantly influenced agreements, such as the Quadripartite Agreement on Berlin, in which they were not even directly represented. At all times, they consulted closely with the United States, even if they did not fully agree.

Soviet policy also played a role. The Soviet Union during the Cold War and detente pursued similar or at least compatible policies toward the United States and the Federal Republic. These Soviet attitudes helped the Western Alliance to coordinate its own policies. They also helped Moscow achieve detente by helping create coordinated policies in the West.

Differences in focus of respective German and American negotiations with the Soviet Union led the two states to different evaluations of detente. The situation along central European borders was relatively stable, although ugly incidents along the Berlin Wall and along the East-West German boundary took place from time to time and had an impact on German public opinion. Even the salami slices that the Soviet Union and East Germany attempted in Berlin for some years were aimed more at American, British, and French than direct West German interests. However, the Soviet Union continued to expand its strategic arsenal at a pace worrisome to the United States. Growing Soviet adventurism in Angola, Ethiopia and Yemen deeply troubled American public opinion and the American government. Therefore, the Germans and the Americans looked upon the detente experience differently. The Germans believed that detente worked in certain areas of crucial direct interest to them, even as they recognized that Soviet behavior outside Europe could not be ignored. Under the general umbrella of detente, the Federal Republic was able to negotiate a series of agreements with the German Democratic Republic. Those agreements, which generally offered West German money in exchange for relaxation of travel and communications restrictions as well as for improved civilian land and water access to Berlin, expanded ties between the two German states. Those arrangements were broadly welcomed in the Federal Republic, despite some reservations about their cost, as a means of improving communications between divided families and of easing access to Berlin. There are indications, perhaps genuine, that the Soviet Union may be concerned that such agreements not go too far in developing an all-German dialogue that excludes Moscow.

Differences in German and American attitudes could be seen in such matters as human rights. Bonn generally—in the context of the CSCE Agreements and in its own direct relations with Eastern Europe—defined human rights differently from Washington. Germany stressed the human right to travel. Millions of Germans every year travel from West Germany and West Berlin to East Germany and East Berlin. Some East Germans, usually elderly or politically suspect, come west. Fifty thousand immigrants of German origin, mainly from Poland, come to West Germany every year to join relatives or to be among fellow-Germans. Although this travel is often linked to German trade and credits, it represents to many Germans whose families have been divided a positive benefit of detente. In contrast, the United States in recent years stressed in human rights the freedom of political activity. Washington criticized Soviet persecution of political dissidents.

The Germans believed that human rights matters could only be handled discreetly with the Soviet Union. The United States chose to address them openly in order to create a compelling climate of world opinion for greater human rights. This tactical difference, as well as differences in stress on various human rights, complicated German-American coordination in policy toward the Soviet Union, specifically within the framework of CSCE, and posed some problems in German-American relations.

All these issues faded into the background in December 1979. The Soviet invasion of Afghanistan brought home the perils of the post-detente era as well as the complexities of coordinating an allied response to Soviet actions. The United States reacted swiftly and strongly, sharply curtailing grain sales to the Soviet Union, further limiting exports of high-technology goods, and indicating that it planned to boycott the 1980 Moscow Olympics. President Carter pledged that the United States would view a Soviet threat to the Persian Gulf as a threat to its own security and would protect its interests, if necessary by military means. He moved to expand the U.S. military presence in the area, and he asked the U.S. Congress to resume registration for the draft.

The United States asked for alliance solidarity in reacting to the Soviet invasion. The Federal Republic affirmed its solidarity, stating that it would act in accordance with what it termed a "division of labor." Under that concept, the German government said that it would not match U.S. military deployment to the Persian Gulf but would greatly increase its aid to Turkey, Greece, and Pakistan. It pledged to raise its security budget, without specifying exactly how this would increase its military strength. It did not match the U.S. draft registration since German forces already functioned on the basis of a draft. It implied, however, that it would be prepared to shoulder a bigger European defense burden if American forces currently stationed in Europe had to be sent to the Persian Gulf. It stressed that the Soviet invasion represented a challenge in the first instance to the nations of the Third World. It did not restrict trade against the Soviet Union, since that trade represented a significantly greater share of Gross National Product for Germany than for the United States and since Germany relied on the Soviet Union for certain essential raw materials, but it pledged not to undercut the American boycott.

While working with the United States, Germany also consulted with other European countries. Schmidt visited Giscard for a regular Franco-German consultation. The meeting produced a communique that condemned Soviet actions and affirmed the solidarity of both partners within the Atlantic alliance. That communique and subsequent European Community statements established a European position not so much different as separate from the American, though also divergent in several respects. The sum of these European reactions produced expressions of concern from the United States, questioning whether the European allies were really supporting the United States in the crisis, especially in the light of even greater European than American dependence of Persian Gulf petroleum.

Although these issues were ultimately resolved, the Afghanistan crisis brought into focus some of the different interpretations and evaluations that had been developing for some time with respect to the purpose and achievements of detente and with respect to East-West relations as a whole. The Germans and Americans agreed that detente was incompatible with the Soviet notion that ideological and world power competition could continue at all times and by all methods. They differed, however, because of their various situations, about the methods they chose to show their disapproval of Soviet actions. Moreover, it took some time for the process of mutual consultation to function effectively.

The Afghanistan crisis raised several broader German-American issues:

— How Germany and America could coordinate their policies, even when those policies were and had to be different, in order best to achieve a common objective without damaging their relationship. Their positions could not be identical, though both states wished to be mutually supportive, and the differences initially appeared more important than the parallels. Both clearly expected from each other a measure of immediate support and understanding that took time to develop.

— To what degree joint consultations meant co-responsibility for each other's actions. The Germans wished to be consulted, preferably in advance, about American actions, yet they could not stress this without being ready to share responsibility for those actions to some degree. The Americans wanted German cooperation, yet they could not ask this without giving the Germans an opportunity to participate in planning. The implications of this complex relationship were only slowly understood by all the parties concerned, and clearly remain to be evaluated over time.

Soviet policies toward Washington and Bonn can also complicate relations between Germany and America. Whereas, during the Cold War and detente, the Soviet Union had treated the United States and the Federal Republic in the same way, the U.S.S.R. has begun in the last few years to differentiate its attitudes. When Soviet relations with Washington appeared to deteriorate, the Soviet Union attempted to improve its relations with the Federal Republic. This was clearly evident in the spring of 1977, after the new American administration had approached Moscow with a new SALT proposal and had been rebuffed by the Soviet Union. The Soviets subsequently made a determined effort to improve relations with Bonn. Travel between East and West Germany became easier. More trade agreements were offered. Soviets and East Germans evidently tried to avoid incidents at the Wall. The number of shootings dropped. The new Soviet policies culminated in 1978 in the visit of Leonid Brezhnev to Bonn, followed by the appointment to Bonn of a senior Soviet diplomat, Vladimir Semenov, with a reputation as a former advocate of German unity. Moscow was clearly treating Germany as more of an independent partner. After relations with Washington improved with the signing of SALT II in spring, 1979, Moscow appeared to lose some of its interest in Bonn, only to renew it later in the year.

In the wake of the Western reaction to the Afghan crisis, it was uncertain whether and how Moscow would attempt to divide the United States from its European allies and, specifically, from the Federal Republic. The Germans did not wish to have the Afghan conflict jeopardize for Europe and Germany the achievements of detente. Several German leaders clearly stated this. Schmidt said that he was still prepared to meet with Brezhnev during 1980 as planned, and he as well as other West German officials remained ready to hold scheduled meetings with other East European leaders. However, the Soviets themselves postponed the Schmidt-Brezhnev meeting and other East European countries followed suit, presumably under Soviet pressure. Soviet public statements initially warned that the Federal Republic and other West European countries were jeopardizing detente in Europe by associating themselves with American measures against Moscow. Some Soviet officials hinted darkly that this might mean an increase in tension around Berlin as well as a threat to the kinds of inner-German contacts that detente had gained. If Americans complained that the Germans were not showing enough solidarity with the United States, the Soviets also complained that the Germans were not showing enough resistance to the United States.

Much depended on whether Moscow continued to pursue a course that might lead to simultaneous confrontations in Eurorope and in the Middle East, or whether it might try to split America and Europe by adopting a more conciliatory tone toward the Europeans. Although the Soviets in the first month after their Afghanistan invasion pursued a hard line toward Europe and Germany as toward America, the trends of Soviet policy since 1977 suggested that Moscow would ultimately adopt a softer tone in order to exploit and promote European-American differences.

There are clear reasons why Moscow might want good relations with Bonn. Moscow wants Western trade, technology and continued credits. It wants to influence the German domestic dialogue. It also wants to keep Germany from developing closer ties with China. In addition, the Soviets may regard the Germans as an important link to the West in case relations with the United States deteriorate further. The Soviets would also hope in the process to create friction between the United States and the Federal Republic to weaken NATO.

Another, more complex, Soviet objective may emerge in the context of NATO plans for theater nuclear force modernization. The Soviets may want to begin talks on strategic security matters with the Germans, or at least to influence German attitudes within NATO. It is not yet clear whether they would do this themselves or through East German offices. The Soviets may try to affect German attitudes since the Federal Republic plays a growing role in NATO strategic decision processes and would, additionally, be a key stationing area for modernized Western theater forces. The Soviet Union had tried to place limits on cruise missiles in their negotiations with the United States in SALT II. Having failed, except in a protocol that is scheduled to expire before SALT II, they may now wish to attempt to forestall introduction of those missiles in Europe by talks with the Germans.

This would change the very nature of Soviet-German discussions by bringing strategic issues to the forefront. Such discussions, or even proposals for such discussions, pose the priorities of defense against detente. In effect, they raise the question whether Moscow will try to suggest that Bonn cannot have detente if it persists in a strong defense. Moscow knows that Germany has a strong interest in keeping the benefits it has derived from reduced tensions and from stability in central Europe. Moreover, stability gives the Germans the opportunity again to have good relations with all Eastern European countries, reflecting German desire to overcome some of the barriers that now split the old continent. The Germans, cannot, however, afford to give up their security relations with the West. Those security relations are the genuine foundations of European peace and stability.

It is worth recalling the unspoken principles on which the division of Germany and Europe has developed: If Germany were to be divided, the western portion could be strong; if Germany were to be united, all Germany would be weak. This was the Faustian bargain reflected in the Soviet and Polish proposals of the 1950s. The Federal Republic chose to be part of the West, and rearmed. In trying to contain and limit Western arms, the Soviet Union wants the best of both principles: a divided Germany, and a weak West Germany.

Close examination of these principles poses a related question: Would Moscow offer unity in order to have Germany weak again, and would the Federal Republic accept? The limits on all parties are also evident here. It is an historical truth that German and Russian agreements have generally been made to the disadvantage of the states lying between them. Since the GDR and Poland play a significant part in the Soviet security glacis, Moscow has to be very careful how far it goes. By the same token, the Federal Republic has obtained, albeit at the price of division, unprecedented combinations of security and prosperity for Germans in the West as well as some benefits even for Germans living in the East. These achievements are not to be surrendered lightly.

Even if German unity is not now evidently in the Soviet interest, *talk* of German unity may offer some tactical benefits. It can create some doubt within West Germany, and even more doubt among Germany's allies about what the Germans might do. The Soviets have already begun tentatively playing with this topic by implying that Germany missed a great "opportunity" in the 1950s. They may well step up this campaign to exploit its divisive potential, although they have to exercise some restraint because of the combination of hope and fear that such suggestions can raise in Poland, East Germany, and elsewhere in Eastern Europe. Even Soviet tactical maneuvers, like its diplomatic initiatives, are circumscribed.

If Moscow tries hard to improve ties with Europe and especially with West Germany. Bonn would find it difficult to deal with Moscow during a period of great Washington-Moscow tension, for domestic as well as alliance reasons, but it could not reject Soviet advances out of hand. It could even play a helpful role for the West as a whole by preventing a complete East-West rupture, but German-American relations would be strained.

The dilemma for the Germans lies in the realm of international stability. The Germans, like the Americans, are committed to stability. If anything, they want it even more after two world wars, several economic upheavals, and untold millions of dead, dispossessed, and dislocated. The Soviet Union appears to be practicing selective stability policies, favoring stability in Europe while exploiting and even fomenting disruption elsewhere. It is to German and American advantage to maintain peace in Europe, unless that peace becomes merely a device by which the Soviet Union builds its power both there and elsewhere, but it is easy to differ in evaluating Soviet purposes. The Germans, in particular, will be reluctant to see European stability disrupted in reaction to events elsewhere.

In the new era, management of relations with the Soviet Union will continue to complicate German-American relations. Both Germany and the United States have certain interests in good relations with the East, although each concentrates its relations on different issues. They cannot jeopardize each other's interests. Some have said that Germany must conduct a "balancing act" between East and West. This is misleading. The Federal Republic is a part of the West, just as the United States is, and the evenhandedness suggested by the phrase "balancing act" would be inappropriate for either partner. Like the United States, the Federal Republic performs a balancing *function* toward the East, but its effectiveness in this role depends on its solidarity with the West. What Washington and Bonn have found in the past, and need to retain, is a common policy that manages relations with Moscow in ways that mutually reinforce rather than undercut each other.

The West and the World

The Federal Republic has a growing role to play not only in East-West relations but also in relations among Western nations with the world at large. This role emerged strongly in the early 1970s. Before then, the Germans concentrated primarily upon affairs at home and in Europe. Beyond those areas, the United States was regarded as the champion of German interests, with the world economic and security system led by the United States essentially supplying Germany's needs. West Germany developed extensive trade relations with many countries, but abstained from political involvement. Its policy was based largely on the Hallstein Doctrine, under which it would break relations with any state that recognized East Germany. The West Germans perceived world events in the mirror of their own immediate concerns near home and saw no reason for any independent or significant world role.

This situation changed in the late 1960s and early 1970s. The United States, for a variety of reasons, was less able to protect German interests internationally. Raw materials problems, especially high petroleum prices and potential crude petroleum shortages, became a dominant factor in German thinking after the 1973 Arab-Israeli war and the drastic oil price hike that same year. Germany was also free, by detente, of the constraints of the Hallstein Doctrine. It could and did move more freely and energetically on the international scene. Germany felt both able and compelled to play a greater international role, not only economically but also politically.

Despite expanding German freedom to act in world affairs, the Federal Republic has tended to move on the world scene largely in concert with partners in the European Community (EC). This suits the German desire to maintain a low profile. It has also made it easier for the Germans, as Europeans, to take positions that they could not take on their own, particularly in the Middle East. As might be expected, German policies in the world as a whole still concentrate heavily on economic relations, but they have also developed through the EC and separately a notable political content.

The principal instrument for EC collaboration in political affairs abroad has been the European Political Cooperation (EPC) formula, first developed by the EC in 1969. That cooperation was considerably strengthened after the 1973 Middle East war and during the "Year of Europe" stimulated by the United States. The European Council developed statements on "the European identity," the Middle East, CSCE, Portugal, and on many other topics. In 1974 it developed a formula for better economic relations with Arab countries, called the "Euro-Arab Dialogue," to improve European chances of continuing to obtain Middle East oil. The Federal Republic played a prominent role within the EC in the development and expansion of the political coordination of the Community. That role was most prominent in EC policy to help support democratic forces in Spain and Portugal, as well as in the opening of a political dialogue between the EC and the states of the Association of Southeast Asian Nations (ASEAN), a dialogue which began late in 1978.

German policy as part of the EC occasionally put the Federal Republic in delicate situations toward the United States, when a majority of EC states wanted to pursue policies different from America's. In those instances, the Germans tried to play a mediating role, not abandoning EC policies but attempting to shape them in order to reduce actual or potential conflict with American policy. They played this role particularly with respect to the "Year of Europe" and the 1973 war, when the Federal Republic, more than any other European state, provided support for American policy. Sharp differences did arise in 1973, however, over shipments to Israel of U.S. military equipment stored on German territory. On other occasions, the Germans were proud when European policies that they supported appeared more successful than they thought American policies would have been. They believed this to be true, and said so, regarding their policies toward southern Europe, most specifically Portugal.

The Germans were clearly embarrassed during the "Year of Europe" by conflicts between the United States and the EC. To help end such conflicts, the Germans proposed a system for closer political consultation between the Community and the United States. This system—known as the "Gymnich Formula" after the castle near Bonn where it was adopted by the 1974 EPC Ministerial Meeting—has eased potential conflict. It has provided a framework for frank, intimate, and continuous working level consultation between the United States and the EC through the rotating presidency of the Community. It can help resolve basic differences of view, since it improves coordination and mutual confidence.

The Federal Republic, having a European and an Atlantic vocation while also depending on the United States in strategic matters, probably feels more keenly than other European states any frictions between European and American policies. However, while attempting to develop a European consensus that will not create a rift with the United States, Germany also wants not to be perceived either as Washington's "Trojan Horse" in Europe or as Europe's directing power. The result has been, and will continue to be, difficult maneuvering. On the other hand, the Germans insist that this maneuvering has helped the Atlantic relationship as a whole because it has not only influenced European but also American policies and has brought them closer together. The Germans attempted to play such a role during the Afghanistan crisis as well.

German world policy has not, however, always operated as part of the European Community. In some areas the Federal Republic has acted on its own. The sale of German civilian nuclear technology abroad represents a particular German interest that has generated, and promises to continue to generate, friction with the United States. This industry was regarded by the Germans in the 1960s and early 1970s as a key element in their concerted strategy to stay at the forefront of international technology exports. After 1973, the Germans also saw the industry as a vehicle to greater energy and economic independence.

The Germans sold nuclear power plants to a number of states. The most important contract, valued at about $5 billion, was for the sale to Brazil of a reprocessing plant and a uranium enrichment plant as well as of several nuclear power plants. Signed in 1975, the contract created a sharp crisis in German-American relations in 1977, when the new American administration challenged it as a potential source of proliferation of sensitive nuclear technology and thus perhaps nuclear military capability. The American attitude may also have been influenced by the planned location of the equipment in Latin America, an area of particular United States sensitivity. The Germans insisted on carrying out the terms of the contract, which they believed contained adequate safeguards against proliferation. Then, at American initiative, the International Nuclear Fuel Cycle Evaluation (INFCE) was started. Several states, including the United States and the Federal Republic, participated. A by-product of this study was the easing of German-American strains over the Brazil agreement and related issues. The study gave both countries, as well as others, the opportunity to evaluate different technologies for resistance to proliferation. The study was to be completed by

1980 and may be followed by similar multilateral review mechanisms on a continuing basis since many of the questions raised in the proliferation controversy cannot be permanently or unanimously answered.

American reservations about nuclear proliferation as well as about nuclear energy technology as a whole helped to legitimize the anti-nuclear "Green" movement in Germany. This movement, combined with a lower than predicted rise in German energy requirements, has slowed the development of German nuclear power at home. Paradoxically, it may motivate German nuclear power industry to strive harder for international sales in order to compensate for slowdowns in domestic business. Although the immediate dispute over the sale of German nuclear technology to Brazil subsided after 1977, it appears possible, and even likely, that further German-American disputes in this area will arise.

Despite the German-American disagreement about the German contract with Brazil, both countries share a common interest against proliferation of nuclear military power. They differ on how best to achieve that interest. The United States challenges certain types of contracts that include sensitive technology or equipment exports. The Federal Republic believes that failure to conclude international agreements will increase the likelihood of national efforts without safeguards, and thus increase the risk of proliferation.

The German position on nuclear proliferation generally reflects European views, although there are also differences among European states. These views emerged strongly in Europe's reaction to American legislation in 1978 requiring renegotiation of existing agreements for cooperation. These agreements provide the framework for supply of American nuclear fuel to the European Community. While some European Community members wanted to reject the American legislation and refuse to negotiate, the Federal Republic recommended negotiations and urged them on other EC members. The negotiations constituted another instance in which the Germans, although agreeing with the views of their

European partners more than with the United States, worked successfully to prevent a transatlantic breach.

The nuclear power controversy illustrates how frictions can arise between Bonn and Washington as the German world role expands. To date, differences have been contained, principally because German and American interests in world affairs broadly parallel each other. Various consultative mechanisms and concentrated effort have smoothed out more potential frictions.

Two potential dangers to political coordination loom on the horizon of the relationship:

—If the Germans come to believe that the United States is losing the capacity or the will to protect the interests of the West as a whole in its dealings with the world at large, the Federal Republic would feel obliged to pursue its own policies or, more likely, to concert with the EC on policies different from America's. This, however, does not represent for Germany or the United States an unavoidable necessity or even a preference. Moreover, it is a double-edged question because American capacity to deal with international problems depends more than before on the support of its friends, including Germany.

—If a crisis develops so quickly that the West has no time to reach agreement on the origins and meaning of the crisis, or on how the West should react, the Germans might choose policies that conflict with American policies. Given the unstable world order, such an eventuality is clearly possible and even likely. There have been suggestions for a NATO or NATO-related mechanism to help coordinate alliance policies on crises that affect the Atlantic nations even though they occur outside the formal area of NATO responsibility, but nothing concrete has yet emerged.

Against these potential difficulties, however, remains the basic reality that, whether in East-West relations or in policies toward other world problems, broad German-American interests for stability and peace continue to coincide.

III. SECURITY RELATIONS

Security cooperation between the United States and the Federal Republic of Germany has solved some European and American problems that had long appeared unsolvable. That cooperation has helped bring about peace in Europe for over a generation, almost unprecedented in recorded history.

In the past, Prussia and Germany, lying in the heart of Europe, sought security in superior military forces. Those forces frightened Germany's neighbors into alliances that encircled Germany, provoking a German sense of isolation, a siege mentality, and ultimately the two most destructive wars in history. It was a classic dilemma. Germany could be stronger than any neighbor and still not feel secure. The American guarantee, in conjunction with the NATO umbrella, solved the problem. Germany could feel safe, and *be* safe, without being perceived as threatening.

These arrangements also solved the dilemma that brought America into the two world wars: to avoid having Europe under the domination of a power that could threaten American security interests. By stationing its forces in the heart of Europe, with the concurrence of West European states, the United States could avert the recurrence of such a threat. These mutual contributions—the American nuclear deterrent to German security and the use of German territory as the station for American forces—have provided the basic building blocks for European and world peace since World War II.

These contributions have also affected domestic politics in the two countries. In the past, the need for strong armed

forces stimulated German official objections to free democratic expression that could jeopardize security needs. German defense requirements were asserted against democratic
yearnings within the population and the political system, to
the disadvantage of the latter. For Germany, this is no longer
necessary. For the United States, the existence of an American front line far from home has vastly increased the sense of
safety and security. Thus, for both Germany and America,
the mutual defense relationship contributes significantly to
domestic tranquility.

NATO's role in these arrangements remains crucial. The
Germans could not place their forces under foreign command
were it not an alliance command. American forces could not
be in Europe solely on the basis of bilateral arrangements
with Germany. Moreover, not only American and German,
but other NATO forces as well, defend the central European
front. The totality of the arrangements has given Europe
stability and peace. Germany is secure. Other Western European states feel less threatened by powers East or West. All,
and particularly the United States and Germany, have an
interest in preserving these arrangements.

The arrangements even contain certain benefits for the
Soviet Union, which still expresses fear that German militar-
ism will revive. The presence of American and other Western
forces in Germany and the NATO security guarantee insure
the stability of the central front not only toward the West
but also toward the East. One indirect effect of the German-
American security relation, therefore, is also to preserve for
the Eastern European states the sense that present arrangements guarantee stability. This has not, however, freed the
Soviet Union from the temptation to disrupt NATO.

Within NATO's structure, American and German forces
complement each other. American forces provide the principal nuclear retaliatory capacity. They provide the second
heaviest concentration of troops along the central front.
They also provide extensive logistic support and a capacity

for reinforcement in case of crisis or war. Germany provides the largest single force along the central front. It also provides, for the United States and other NATO nations, maneuver room and stationing arrangements.

Germany neither seeks nor will attain equality with the United States in strategic nuclear capability. The Federal Republic has signed the Nonproliferation Treaty, after a long and intense debate that was neither understood nor appreciated in the United States. Germany's signature on the treaty, in a sense, means indefinite reliance by the Federal Republic on the American security guarantee.

The mutual dependence of the two states introduces an element of considerable sensitivity into German-American security relations. The two states remain constantly alert to each other's policies. The Germans tend to watch American security decisions with intense attention whereas the Americans scrutinize the German contribution to alliance efforts. At the same time, the mutual dependence creates an important, even vital, bond.

Under NATO doctrine, Germany and America have both adopted the strategy of "flexible response," which stresses the ability to meet any Soviet attack at whatever level necessary to repel the attack, preserving NATO freedom to escalate to such level. Since the United States is far from the front line of any possible Soviet conventional attack, although American forces would help to defend that line, the stress in American thinking has always been on the word "flexible," with various elements of NATO tactical and strategic nuclear arsenal being used as appropriate. The Germans have always stressed the word "response," meaning potentially immediate strategic nuclear retaliation. The Germans, whose land would probably be the main battlefield, inevitably put more stress than any other NATO country on the importance of deterrence.

In the post-detente era, security is more complicated than it was during the Cold War or detente. Adequate military power remains essential. However, the diplomatic option always exists as a supplement or alternative. The Harmel Report, adopted by NATO in 1967 and frequently cited since, stressed the importance of regarding military power and detente diplomacy as mutually reinforcing elements of security, as two sides of the same coin. For Germans and Americans, the continuing security priority in the 1980s will be to coordinate military deterrence and diplomacy in order to sustain security and the sense of stability.

Theater Nuclear Force Modernization

Such coordination will be urgently needed to meet a new NATO requirement: the modernization of long-range theater nuclear forces (LRTNF) in Europe. If the common basis for German and American security is to continue, this problem requires solution. There is every indication that it will not be easy.

Theater nuclear forces play an essential role in NATO deterrence doctrine by making clear that the Soviets cannot exploit conventional superiority to win a war in Europe. Theater nuclear forces are intended to permit NATO to go to whatever level is necessary to defeat a Warsaw Pact attack. They cover a wide spectrum of weapons systems, from short-range nuclear artillery all the way to long-range missiles and deep penetration aircraft. They are to be used, if necessary, to help stop any Soviet advance, to make the Soviet and Warsaw Pact forces pay a high price for any attack and—most important in many eyes—to show the kind of determination that would persuade the Soviet Union to pull back rather than persist in its attack.

German ambivalence about defense vis-à-vis deterrence has always been reflected in its attitude toward these weapons. Since German territory—both East and West—could well be the primary battleground for a theater nuclear exchange, the West Germans at first did not favor deployment of nuclear forces in Europe. They preferred conventional defense. When it became clear that fully adequate conventional defense was too costly and might not in itself deter a Soviet attack, West Germany supported theater nuclear forces but only in the hope that they would never have to be used or that, if they were used, it would be as far as possible from German soil.

The Germans want theater nuclear forces to be only the first rung up the ladder of escalation, with that ladder clearly reaching all the way to American strategic intercontinental systems, so that the Soviets will be deterred from attack by fear of rapid escalation up the ladder. The Germans on occasion call TNF systems "Euro-strategic" or "Continental Strategic," in part to underline that these weapons are part of total strategic deterrence and can ignite a global nuclear missile exchange. The Germans believe that only such a risk will deter the Soviet Union. They regard the link—or "coupling"—of American strategic and TNF forces as essential for European security.

The Germans, therefore, desire theater nuclear forces that are strong enough to be taken seriously at any level, but not strong enough to make the Soviets believe that NATO is unlikely to move up to the next level. The Germans want enough TNF weapons so that each escalation rung constitutes a credible defense and a sign of determination to resist, but they do not desire full equivalence at each level. They want forces that can deter even as they defend.

The Americans have a different attitude toward TNF weapons. They are less persuaded than the Germans that the steps up the rung of escalation must appear probable and even automatic. The United States favors the principle of graduated deterrence, interrupted by what have been termed "fire-breaks," with deterrence at every level to remain strong enough to repel a Soviet attack at that level. The fire-breaks must not, however, become too wide.

The Soviet doctrine in some ways parallels the German doctrine and in other ways, the American doctrine. The

Soviets, like the Germans and all Europeans, see Europe as a strategic area and not as a theater. The Soviets believe this not only because they are themselves Europeans but also because weapons that they regard as strategic could be launched against them from European soil. This has been at the foundation of their concern about American forward-based systems (FBS), such as the F-111 bomber, stationed in Europe. Like the United States, however, the Soviets wish to have a continuum of nuclear weapons. They also want to be superior at any level and to be able to decide whether to go higher. Like the United States, they want to be able to control the escalatory ladder. In accordance with that wish, they have developed nuclear systems at all levels and all ranges.

The Soviet Union now appears to have developed a system intended for even greater escalation control, and to be in the process of deploying the system. It is the SS-20, a ballistic missile launcher with a range of over 3,000 miles, with a considerably greater accuracy than any current Soviet LRTNF, and with the specific advantage of mobility. Over 120 launchers had been deployed by spring 1980 in western, central, and eastern Russia, thus covering Europe, the Middle East, and much of Asia.

Deployment of the SS-20 is continuing at the rate of about 50 per year. Most Western estimates anticipate that a total of 250 to 300 will be deployed. Since each missile carries three warheads, completion of the program could add to the Soviet arsenal about 750 to 900 warheads, of perhaps 150 kilotons each, with which to attack targets well beyond the periphery of Soviet territory. The missiles can hit any portion of Western Europe from the western sectors of the Soviet Union. They also can hit parts of NATO territory from most of Soviet territory. If the Soviets decide to assign more than one missile per launcher, the number of warheads can be multiplied.

This SS-20, with its extension of range, accuracy, and capacity, represents a fundamentally new potential. It marks a quantum jump in the development of theater nuclear forces. It dramatically alters the European balance and must be regarded as an instrument for intimidation. It gives the Soviets the option of a devastating first strike or of a second strike, as well as a greater war-fighting capability, since it is mobile and thus has high survivability. Even more important, the SS-20 is accompanied by the deployment of an array of new Soviet shorter-range systems, the SS-21, SS-22, and SS-23. Those systems, deployed in East Germany and Poland, can effectively conduct Soviet theater nuclear operations. The SS-20s would ensure that NATO dare not strike Soviet territory in retaliation. If not countered, the combination of SS-20s and short-range weapons would give Moscow theater nuclear superiority as well as the instrument by which to separate Soviet soil from the conflict. The Soviet Union could thus decouple its own territory and, by implication, all great power territory. This decoupling breaks the escalation ladder, of vital concern to Bonn as well as to NATO doctrine.

In addition to the SS-20, the Soviets have developed and deployed the Backfire, a bomber with a speed of 2.5 mach and a range estimated at about 5,500 miles, enough to attack targets all over Western Europe. By spring 1980, over 160 of these bombers had been deployed. Deployment is continuing at the rate of 30 per year, as limited in a special Soviet obligation related to the SALT II Agreement. Like the SS-20s, the Backfires are not deployed exclusively opposite Western Europe, but also opposite Asia and other parts of the Soviet periphery.

As indicated earlier, German doctrine regarded some TNF imbalance in Europe as acceptable because it would ensure American involvement and thus maintain coupling. This notion was based, however, on the assumption that U.S. central strategic systems could and would be used for deterrence. The arrival of the SS-20 and the negotiations for SALT II altered the assumptions on which German doctrine had been based. The SS-20 widened the TNF imbalance from a gap to a chasm, whereas SALT II, by formalizing intercontinental strategic parity, made the Germans fear that the Soviets would no longer regard U.S. strategic forces as a deterrent. The Germans were afraid that this combination of events could tempt Moscow to seek military dominance and political influence over Western Europe, since Moscow could believe that it might attack without risking retaliation against its own territory. The Soviets could choose when and where to attack, and could decide the level of the conflict; they could feel invulnerable to retaliation because they might think American central systems would not be used and there was little in Western Europe with which to strike back at Russian territory.

In German eyes, the nature of the SALT II agreement as they understood it to be under negotiation made this worse. The Germans feared that in SALT the United States was making sure only that Backfire remained a theater rather than a global weapon, but was not limiting it in any other way. In addition, the Germans feared that the protocol attached to the SALT II Agreement would limit American development and deployment of cruise missiles, a system that the Germans perceived as a possible countermeasure to the SS-20. When several senior Americans in the summer and fall of 1977 predicted the imminent signature of SALT II, the Germans became very concerned.

After German officials raised these issues in discussions with American officials several times, Chancellor Schmidt voiced his concerns in public in October, 1977. Schmidt warned that "strategic arms limitations confined to the United States and the Soviet Union will inevitably impair the security of the West European members of the alliance vis-à-vis Soviet military superiority in Europe, if we do not succeed in removing the disparities of military power in Europe parallel to the SALT negotiations." Schmidt's speech led to intensified consultations between Germans and Americans, as well as toward broader consultations within the entire NATO family. The United States, which had also been concerned about the SS-20 and about other Soviet theater nuclear developments, gradually took the lead in these consultations. NATO began to shape concrete plans for the modernization of LRTNF and for an arms control initiative to try to limit such forces on both sides.

The Federal Republic participated in the NATO consultations. However, although Chancellor Schmidt had been the first senior Western leader to call public attention to the TNF problem, the Germans did not take a similar lead in the consultations. The Germans stressed that it had been their function to call attention to a serious problem, but that the Americans as the senior nuclear partner of the alliance had to lead the way toward a solution. They also said that any solution could not "single out" Germany within the alliance, since Germany was not a nuclear power and could not bear the whole burden of possible Soviet retaliation against the NATO action. The Germans insisted that they would not accept stationing of any LRTNFs on German soil unless at least one other non-nuclear NATO member on the European continent accepted stationing. They further said that they did not wish to have a "key" to the new LRTNF systems deployed on German soil so that decisions about their use were to be exclusively American.

In December, 1979, the NATO Council decided to proceed with LRTNF modernization, subjct to reservations by several countries requiring negotiations with the Soviet Union for LRTNF limitations. Specifically, it decided for production and deployment of the following systems in the following numbers:

—108 Pershing II of extended range (P-2XR)
—116 ground-launched cruise missile launchers, with a total of 464 cruise missiles.

The P-2XR is to be stationed in Germany under full U.S. control. Of the cruise missiles, about 100 are to be stationed in Germany and others in other NATO countries. The current stockpile of nuclear warheads in Western Europe, many in West Germany, is to be reduced so that LRTNF modernization does not increase total NATO dependence on nuclear weapons. The Council also decided that, while production is proceeding, the alliance would attempt to negotiate with the Soviet Union an agreement for limiting and possibly reducing numbers of LRTNF.

The NATO consultations leading up to the December meeting were, as usual, extensively reported in the Western press. They aroused considerable Soviet interest. In order to influence the NATO debate, and perhaps to head off any decision in December, Brezhnev on October 6, 1979, offered NATO both a carrot and a stick. The carrot was a declaration of Soviet readiness to reduce, from the present level, the number of its medium-range missiles deployed in the Western Soviet Union if no additional missiles were deployed in Western Europe. As a demonstration of serious intent, Brezhnev said that the Soviet Union planned to reduce its forces in the GDR by 20,000 soldiers and 1,000 tanks within the next 12 months. As a stick, Brezhnev warned that Western deployment of additional missiles would "change the strategic situation on the continent" and "inevitably aggravate the situation in Europe and in many respects vitiate the international atmosphere in general." He termed the NATO plans as "dangerous." Shortly thereafter, the Soviets began some actual withdrawals of forces from East Germany.

Brezhnev focused considerable attention on Germany. He said the FRG was assigned "not the least part" in the preparation of these plans and added that "those who shape that country's policy are today facing a very serious choice." He warned that deployment of these weapons in Germany would mean that "the position of the FRG itself would considerably worsen." His concentration on Germany was later reinforced in statements by other Soviet officials.

As might be expected, different German officials reacted in different ways to the Soviet statements. There had already been considerable debate in Germany about the wisdom of LRTNF production and deployment, and some Social Democratic Party (SPD) leaders said that deployment of the new weapons should perhaps not be decided until negotiating possibilities had been examined. However, at the SPD Congress in December 1979, the party voiced its support for the government policy to participate in NATO deployment decisions and to use the period before actual deployment to explore arms control possibilities with the Soviet Union.

Soviet statements indicated that at least one of the purposes of the Soviet deployment of new long-range TNF systems was political. The Soviet threat, suggesting that countries that harbor American TNF would be subject to early Soviet retaliation, was reminiscent of Khrushchev's bluster of the 1950s. It confirmed to many Americans and Europeans that some force to balance the new Soviet systems had to be built, since the Soviets appeared to be trying to make superiority permanent. At the same time, the threat showed Soviet intent to exert every means of pressure against a matching Western buildup.

The next few years, while NATO LRTNF systems are being produced and arms control options explored, promise to be diplomatically and politically active. Under present production plans, NATO would be able to deploy modernized TNF by 1983, though site preparation might begin earlier. Soviet threats and enticements in the fall of 1979 probably only foreshadow what is yet to come. Therefore, the upcoming years will present particular challenges to NATO cohesion and, especially, to German-American collaboration.

Assuming these problems can be overcome, with the weapons deployed and/or a meaningful arms control arrangement reached, the alliance should emerge significantly stronger. Just as Moscow had a political purpose in deploying its own system, a NATO response would have clear political content. It would signify that, in the post-detente era, the alliance has the political will and capacity to conduct a combination of defense and diplomacy.

The new NATO long-range TNF systems can achieve significant objectives. Appropriately deployed, they can give NATO a reliable second-strike capability, since the new systems can be mobile and not targetable by Soviet systems. In addition, the new systems should reduce and perhaps end concerns about decoupling, in particular because the Soviets would regard them as strategic weapons. Given those new systems on the European continent as visible evidence of the American strategic nuclear commitment, the Soviet Union could not confidently plan attacks on Europe without anticipating American nuclear involvement and reaction. Deployment of the new weapons would thus meet the concerns expressed by Schmidt in 1977.

While deployment of the new systems can have a positive effect on nuclear stability in Europe, it can present new and difficult challenges to traditional arms control methods. These challenges will require special study within the NATO alliance. It is clear that the alliance will have to make a serious effort to achieve a negotiated limit not only for domestic political reasons but also because it would be more desirable from every standpoint if the TNF balance in Europe could be maintained at a low level.

Arms control arrangements to establish a stable balance between the new NATO systems and the corresponding Soviet systems will, however, require delicate and complicated negotiations with Moscow and prolonged consultations among the allies. A precise balance is difficult to establish. The West will want to negotiate parity in principle even if it does not want exact parity on the ground because of its decoupling implications. The Soviets will reckon not only the new systems but also British, French, and Chinese systems into the balance. Any arrangement will prove difficult to verify, in part because of the mobility of the systems and in part because of their reload capacity.

Divergences in German and American views as to the strategic character of LRTNF systems may also make Germany more amenable than America to Soviet suggestions for a global ceiling that includes both central and theater systems. The West cannot attempt to reduce the threat by insisting on placement of Soviet systems further to the East, in part because mobility reduces the significance of such placement and in part because of the many Western friends and allies in Asia. The negotiators will concentrate on Europe, but the Soviet weapons are designed for operations and political effect along the entire periphery of the Soviet Union.

The Germans, like other Europeans and like the Americans, will have a clear interest in the resolution of all these questions. Bonn and Washington will have to concert closely across the Atlantic and in NATO. Because of different perceptions and attitudes in Germany and the United States on these weapons, it will not be easy to develop positions. Not all the delicate issues are on the Western side, however. The Soviet Union must explain to its allies, especially the GDR and Poland, why NATO theater nuclear forces become such a serious problem when they can hit Russian soil but were tolerable when they could hit other Warsaw Pact states.

Obviously, it would be beyond the scope of this paper to attempt to answer the questions posed by arms control negotiations. What does appear clear, even now, is that imaginative new arms control devices may be required, going well beyond the formulas used in the SALT negotiations. It is not clear what new verification procedures, confidence-building measures, counting rules, or combination of all those, will be effective. The Germans and Americans, along with other NATO partners, will have to play key roles in formulating new concepts. Since German territory and American systems are involved, this will require considerable joint thinking.

A particular dilemma for the Germans, who are interested in moving quickly to substantive negotiations, might be the risk of Soviet stalling tactics. The Soviets may well decide that it is in their best interest to delay serious negotiations because, while the West is still producing its own new theater weapons, the Soviet systems are in place and are continuing to grow in number. Some in Moscow may say that the Soviet Union should not make any real offers at first, but should use negotiations principally to slow down Western deployment since the gap will widen to its advantage for at least two or three more years and must first be exploited rather than negotiated away. It cannot be excluded that, when the gap is at its peak in the early 1980s, and when the United States might also suffer from concerns about strategic vulnerability, the Soviets might increase the threats and pressure tactics that they have already been disposed to show in the fall of 1979.

The Soviets might well concentrate their threats as well as their blandishments on the Federal Republic. Chapter II has already reviewed some of the tactics that the Soviets might attempt with Germany. At a time when their theater superiority appears even greater than it appears now, the Soviets may well accompany such inducements with very stern warnings. In such a case, it would be absolutely essential for the Germans and the Americans to have confidence in each other, since one of the most important purposes of such Soviet tactics would be to drive a wedge between Washington and Bonn.

The LRTNF problem, in its strategic and diplomatic implications, again dramatically underlines the special German vulnerabilities resulting from Germany's division as well as from its position in the center of Europe. At the same time, it gives greater weight to Germany in alliance decision making. Even if the Germans do not want it, they cannot change the reality of their expanded responsibility. Schmidt recognized this when he said, in February 1980, that without German support no decision to modernize LRTNF would have been possible. The Germans will have no role in the handling of any nuclear hardware, but they will have a highly prominent role in the consultations on the diplomacy and on the deployment of the new systems. For the first time since World War II, the Germans will be negotiating on a strategic matter with the Soviet Union. Depending on the forum ultimately chosen for the talks, they may be doing this directly or indirectly, but they will be unable to avoid that role.

The Soviets always have had particular sensitivities about German armed forces and about weapons stationed in Germany, perhaps as a result of their historic respect for German ingenuity and organizational ability as well as out of their experiences of the last two world wars. This concern should have been erased by the German decision not to seek a "key" to the new LRTNF systems, but it may well not be totally dispelled.

The Soviet attitude is also reflected in the MBFR negotiations. There, the Soviets appear at least as much determined to place a ceiling on German forces as to negotiate American force reductions. The Germans have been very conscious of this Soviet purpose. They have also expressed concern that elements in the MBFR negotiations might lead Germany to become a "special zone" for arms control arrangements, thus weakening Germany's ability to participate fully in NATO, and they have indicated an interest in recent French disarmament proposals because they suggest a wider zone of European arms control. Those attitudes will also be evident in the TNF negotiations.

Pressures for arms control particularly affect the SPD. TNF modernization represents the first major weapons program of a nuclear character involving the Federal Republic since the SPD entered the German government. In the past, the Social Democrats have rather opposed than sponsored arms programs, yet the party in government cannot fail to accept the responsibility for defending Germany. The opposition can charge that the SPD cannot keep Germany secure.

On the other hand, if the party is to remain united, all elements must be persuaded that arms control alternatives have been genuinely and thoroughly explored.

The United States also will feel certain pressures in those negotiations. Arms control has become a key element of American security planning. Given the link between the TNF negotiations and the continuation of any strategic arms control process, the United States will also have an interest in the success of the TNF negotiations and, should they fail, in at least being able to show that a genuine effort was made. However, coordination on specifics will not be easy.

These are the realities of the new post-detente era. Strategic needs and diplomatic requirements intersect at complex angles. Decisions cannot be made quickly or easily, whether in Western capitals or in the Soviet Union. All participants need to keep in mind not only their own and their Cold War antagonists' actions, but also the interests and possible reaction of countries not in the respective alliance systems.

Just as Germany and the United States entered the Cold War and detente together, so they have together entered the tangled strategic realm of the post-detente era. It will require the most careful and precise coordination of policy within the framework of the NATO systems. It will also require enormous reserves of mutual confidence. At crucial points both countries, like many of their NATO colleagues, will perceive even more clearly how they rely on each other for the most basic security requirements.

Other Defense Issues

While LRTNF modernization represents a momentous potential problem and opportunity for NATO and for German-American cooperation over the next several years, a number of other security matters will require the close attention of NATO planners as well as of Washington and Bonn defense officials. All these matters require financial as well as military decisions, with each step to be taken costing money for one or more allies. Space limitations preclude more than a terse outline of each issue, but some of the principal German-American implications are listed below.

Rapid Reinforcement.

To implement the strategy of forward defense and compensate for greater Warsaw Pact conventional forces, plans are being developed for the rapid deployment of three American divisions to Europe at times of tension or conflict. In order to avoid using scarce logistical assets to carry supplies and equipment for these divisions, those supplies and equipment are to be prepositioned in Europe. Germany would represent a logical place for considerable prepositioning but many questions need to be resolved, including site selection, financing, and other logistical arrangements.

NATO Budget Increases.

In 1977, the 13 NATO nations decided in a non-binding pledge to commit themselves to annual security budget increases of 3 percent in real terms through 1983. Some NATO states have generally adhered to this pledge, but not all have done so. The 1980 German budget did not achieve that rate initially. The United States urged Germany to increase its budget, with the Germans replying that the most important part of the budget, i.e., investment items, were increasing by a larger percentage share and that Bonn would not increase military wages inordinately in order to fatten the budget as the Germans claimed other NATO states have done. Only in response to the Soviet invasion of Afghanistan did the Germans raise their security budget by more than 3 percent.

Standardization of NATO Weapons.

For several years there has been a concerted drive to solve a traditional NATO problem: the multiplicity of types and styles of NATO equipment and supplies, as well as the operational incompatibility between them. The United States, which for a long time supplied a great deal of NATO equipment and, especially, equipment for the German armed forces, has strongly supported this program in principle. It has urged European arms manufacturers to cooperate in developing new weapons systems so that they would be technologically and economically competitive with American production and there could be greater mutual trade of weapons with each country specializing in certain lines of equipment.

The European states have cooperated more than before, with the Germans involved in cooperative arrangements with several large European NATO states and, in turn, collaborating with those states to enable smaller countries also to participate in production. However, many of these arrangements have not led to lower production costs and have not, in American eyes, been at the forefront of technology.

Germany and the United States have also attempted to collaborate on a number of weapons production programs, most notably a common new 120-mm gun, of German design, for new tanks being developed separately by the two states. The negotiations for selection of the German gun by American forces, as well as for the production in America under license, proved lengthy and controversial. Other cooperative ventures will undoubtedly be attempted, but will undoubtedly also be difficult to arrange. Such problems have not altered Bonn's or Washington's commitment to the basic goal of greater weapons standardization. Intra-European collaboration has, however, developed faster than European-American collaboration. This can complicate transatlantic relations by squeezing out U.S. producers.

The Condition of American Forces in Germany.

The rise of the German D-Mark against the U.S. dollar (see Chapter IV) has depressed the standard of living of over 300,000 American servicemen and dependents stationed in Germany, especially at the lower levels of the enlisted grades for whose dependents the U.S. government does not provide transportation or housing. This has, in some cases, provoked genuine hardship. German and American authorities have attempted to ease the problem. One consequence of the lower dollar exchange rate is that American servicemen and their families have fewer opportunities to meet Germans and to participate in German activities, long regarded by both countries as one of the positive benefits of having American forces stationed in Germany.

No single one of these defense issues is central enough to disrupt German-American relations, but they carry political weight beyond their substantive significance. They can quickly arouse emotions on both sides since they involve money, jobs, and national prestige. Those emotions can affect resolution of other issues. However, in each of these problem areas, German and American interests coincide. Both countries want to preserve the strongest possible defense structures at the lowest possible price and on the basis of the closest possible cooperation. In practice, while specific policies have diverged, Bonn and Washington have generally been able to settle these kinds of issues to their mutual appears beyond resolution.

IV. ECONOMICS

S ome economists attempt to convey the impression that theirs is an exact science. Instead, it is a science haunted by ghosts, ghosts of policies past and, particularly, of failures past.

In the German-American economic relationship, and particularly in the international monetary relationship that dominates the current economic scene, Germany and America are haunted by different ghosts, coming from opposite directions. The ghost haunting Germany is that of the Great Inflation of 1923, which destroyed the German middle class financially and helped pave the way for the rise of Hitler. During that inflation, Germans paid billions of marks for the most simple necessities. A quart of milk, for example, cost 15 billion marks. The German mark, worth eight to the dollar in 1919, had collapsed to an exchange rate of 4,200,000,000,000 to one dollar at the peak of Germany's inflation.

German political figures and German economists speak of this inflation as the dominant experience of their lives or their studies. Even the Great Depression, in which 6 million Germans were unemployed, has not made such a profound impression on the thinking of Germany. Moreover, the German phobia about inflation was reinforced by three more years of rapid price rises after World War II, when American cigarettes and Parker pens became the most stable and sought-after units of exchange.

Americans, on the other hand, are haunted by the Great Depression. In their minds, they have pictures of bread lines, of apple salesmen, and of destitute unemployed. Modern

American economic policies have been created largely in reaction to the Great Depression. Americans have not experienced, in their own lives or in the history lessons that dominate their thinking, a prolonged period of sharp inflation. At least, not until now.

German economic thinking is also influenced heavily by Germany's export orientation. The entire economy hinges on maintaining exports. About one quarter of the jobs in German industry depend directly on exports. Most large German industries rely, to the extent of a third or more of their sales, on the export market. They are acutely conscious of the need to remain internationally competitive. German businessmen and entrepreneurs, as well as German workers, think in terms of their ability to compete on the international market.

The United States is a continent. It used to be almost entirely self-sufficient as a producing and market economy. Most American industries and most American workers have been trained to think not in terms of exports but in terms of production for the domestic market. They have, until recently, been less attuned to foreign markets, although they may on occasion become acutely sensitive to foreign competition for the American market. For past decades, the United States has consistently been most competitive in its agricultural goods, although several industrial producers have remained strong. Some of the most advanced American industry has tended not to export from American production but to invest abroad for production in other countries. Whereas the German economy is deliberately geared to the world economy and toward remaining competitive in an international environment, the American economy, at least until recently, has been principally directed to domestic sales.

There are three other important differences between the American and the German economy. First, Germany has had an aging and declining domestic labor supply. This has put a premium on the arrival in Germany of foreign workers, who have numbered between 2 and 3 million. Many leave for their home countries when they lose their jobs, thus not swelling German unemployment rolls. The American economy has had a growing labor supply, for which it must develop jobs. Only in the last few years has the German domestic labor supply risen. Second, in Germany the role of the central bank, the *Bundesbank*, is more independent and influential than the role of a central bank in virtually any other country. Bankers tend toward conservative policies. Third, many German economic decisions and policies are carried out within the framework of the European Community. Many German-American economic issues are also issues between the EC and the United States, or within the EC. Germany's Community role influences, though it does not determine, German policy.

German and American economic philosophy and policy reflect both the ghosts and the realities. German economic philosophy mirrors the doctrines of the Austrian and the monetarist schools of economics. It stresses value, stability, and savings as the sources of growth, and full employment, and the virtue of careful husbanding of resources. American economic philosophy, basic to American economic policies, focuses on the demand stimulation element of Keynesian thinking. It attempts to keep up the demand side of the domestic equation in order to provide full employment. The contrast between German and American doctrine is the stress on value and stability, in part to keep a world competitive position, as against growth in demand, to maintain domestic full employment.

The pattern of German thinking introduces into German policy what Americans regard as a bias toward deflationary policies; American experience and American thinking introduce what the Germans regard as a bias toward inflation.

German-American Monetary Relations

In the decades immediately after World War II, differences in German and American economic philosophy and policy did not matter much. Germany's rebuilding process produced rapid economic growth. American policy, although domestically oriented, generated international prosperity and progress. It set the tone for international as well as domestic policy in many countries. Even those American dollar exports, later so reviled in German and other European thinking, were essential for the liquidity that financed international trade. The Bretton Woods System, created in 1944 at the height of American power, functioned effectively. During the 1940s, 1950s, and early 1960s, moreover, the United States pursued policies more oriented toward stability and toward controlled growth than in the period beginning in the mid-1960s.

Since those years, the history of German-American economic relations has become to a considerable extent the history of various attempts to manage the effects upon the international system, and upon the relationship between the dollar and the D-Mark, of the contrasts between German and American economic and financial policies. The differences between those policies have led to a steady strengthening of the German position in the international monetary picture. They have also led to a steady rise of the D-Mark against the dollar and against virtually all other major currencies.

The Germans revalued the D-Mark in 1961 and again in 1969. Between those revaluations, they helped, in a variety of specific arrangements with the United States and with other countries, to support the dollar. Some of those arrangements were linked to the cost of maintaining U.S. forces in Germany and were known as "offset." Germany bought and held U.S. monetary instruments. It committed itself to government procurement of certain quantities of specific U.S. exports. It participated in a central bank swap network. In addition, Germany did not, as some other countries did, exchange any large part of its dollar reserves for gold. It explicitly gave up the right to do so. By those policies, Germany helped to avoid more frequent revaluations of the D-Mark and to sustain the international system based upon the Bretton Woods arrangement.

Even these measures no longer continued to work by the early 1970s. Dollars, in large quantities, began to flood the exchange markets. Many countries used surplus dollars to buy other currencies, in most cases the D-Mark. The *Bundesbank* tried for some time to purchase dollars in order to maintain their value. However, by May, 1971, it stopped, thus precipitating the era of floating rates. Three months later, on August 15, 1971, the U.S. broke the dollar-gold link by no longer permitting the dollar to be freely convertible to gold. It subsequently began efforts to move from Bretton Woods to a new international monetary system. In the December Smithsonian Agreement, the D-Mark was revalued by almost 14 percent against the U.S. dollar. Even this arrangement was not to last. In April 1972, the members of the European Community introduced the "snake," a joint float of their currencies. Since then, most currencies of the Western industrial world have floated against each other. The D-Mark has consistently remained among the strongest currencies.

In the new floating world, inflation rates among the industrialized nations have continued to vary widely, as have growth rates. Several economic summits, at which both the United States and the Federal Republic played important roles, have attempted to coordinate policy, with only partial success. After 1975, the American economy grew at a faster rate than the German, adding 10 million new jobs where the German economy added virtually none. This was accompanied, in the United States, by a growing inflation rate after 1977. U.S. inflation hit double digit figures in 1979. German inflation generally remained below 5 percent, though it also climbed somewhat in 1979.

This inflation differential has been the principal factor weakening the dollar against the D-Mark. The new floating environment has given political and monetary institutions in both countries greater leeway to follow the economic policies they wanted. Given differing German and American policies, the D-Mark has proven stronger than the dollar, and the floating environment has highlighted and increased the German role and influence. As often happens, the trend has been reinforced by psychological factors, with confidence in the D-Mark growing as it kept rising, and confidence in the dollar declining.

The strengthening of the D-Mark has disturbed the German government and the *Bundesbank* somewhat. They have expressed concern about a weakening of Germany's international trading position if the D-Mark became too strong. However, Germany has also benefited from the strength of its currency. A rising currency has helped enable the German government to keep inflation under control. Moreover, since international petroleum prices are denominated in dollars, a stronger D-Mark has meant that Germany has not felt the impact of higher oil prices as much as have the United States and most other countries. The stronger currency has also helped German prestige internationally and reinforced the domestic position of the government. Thus, the Germans have found themselves in what is sometimes termed a "virtuous circle." They have little incentive to have the dollar appreciate.

One reason why the Germans need not concern themselves about a loss of exports caused by the rise of the D-Mark is that the rate of inflation in Germany's main trading partners has compensated for the D-Mark rise. D-Mark revaluations raise the prices of German goods when expressed in foreign currencies, but those goods remain competitive because domestic inflation has not driven up German production costs as much as it has those in other countries. Germany can compensate for the strong D-Mark by a lower inflation rate, and its competitive position remains undiminished. It is only when the D-Mark rises too fast, because of market mechanics or speculation, that Germany cannot compensate.

Despite whatever benefits the German government and *Bundesbank* may have gained from a stronger D-Mark, it has been clear that Germany would suffer from a precipitous decline of the dollar which would destabilize the entire international system. Therefore, the Germans have continued to cooperate in a variety of measures to limit the decline of the dollar. In 1978 and 1979, the Germans helped by participating in a "swap" package and by permitting the United States to sell so-called "Carter Bonds" in West Germany. The bonds represented useful instruments for both countries. The United States acquired D-Marks to help defend the dollar. In Germany, the bonds soaked up liquidity and helped restrain inflation.

The Germans also influenced American policy against inflation. The actions taken by the U.S. Federal Reserve Bank in October, 1979, raising U.S. reserve requirements and taking other steps that led to higher interest rates, came in part in reaction to German policies and policy views. American Federal Reserve authorities would probably have had to take the actions to meet American domestic needs for a firmer policy against inflation, but German insistence on strong American policies, as well as the monetary climate created by German policy, helped persuade U.S. authorities upon this course.

The Future of Economic Relations

These events have spotlighted Germany's role as a key power on the international financial scene. Germany is now setting policy not only for itself but also for others, in Western Europe and elsewhere. The D-Mark has become the principal instrument of intervention for the protection of the dollar. The Germans are not only telling the Americans how to deal with problems that face the American and the world economy, but they are also creating conditions that compel the United States and other countries to react. Germans see themselves as the principal defenders of what remains of the system that was created 35 years ago by the United States, as well as of the system that succeeded it.

Several elements of German economic power make this possible. The stress on value and stability in German economic thinking makes German currency the strongest currency in a floating system. Germany now has the world's largest currency reserves, almost $50 billion in total, as well as the second-largest gold reserves. The D-Mark has become a store of value and safe haven. At least 10 percent, perhaps 15 percent, of world currency reserves are held in D-Marks.

A fundamental dichotomy complicates German attitudes. The German government and the *Bundesbank* want a strong D-Mark and will do what is necessary to bring this about, if necessary by making certain that other currencies do not appreciate against the D-Mark. At the same time, the Germans do not want the D-Mark to be a major reserve currency. They fear that such a role for the D-Mark would limit their ability to make economic policy on the basis of their domestic requirements and traditional philosophy. It would also lose them some of the benefits they now get from consistent strength against the dollar. This concern led to German reservations about the American decision in November, 1979, to freeze Iranian assets in U.S. banks. The Germans feared that the freeze would drive more oil money into D-Marks and perhaps lead to oil pricing in D-Marks or in a basket of currencies including D-Marks.

There is a similar contradiction in American attitudes. The United States has benefited from the world role of the dollar and does not want to give up those benefits. It wishes to share some of the burdens of that role, but it fears that other countries with whom it would share that burden might not pursue the kinds of policies that the United States thinks in the best interests of the American economy and the international economic system. Like the Germans, the American monetary authorities do not want outside developments or the policies of other countries to make domestic objectives unattainable.

The growing German power in international monetary affairs raises a number of issues that can affect the tone of German-American relations. One problem, for both countries, is to deal with the effects of the phases of economic activity in which they may both find themselves at any given time. This problem of phasing has been a key issue in international monetary affairs during the postwar years. For a long time, Germany and the United States were in phase, having virtually simultaneous waves of growth and recession. During those years, many economists and political figures worried about what was known as the "simultaneity problem," by which respective phases of growth and recession reinforced each other and led to excessive growth or excessive decline. Since 1976, however, the United States and Germany have been out of phase. U.S. growth developed at a rapid rate, whereas German growth was slower. By 1980, the United States may be in a recession phase whereas Germany may continue growth. This problem of being in different phases may not be as severe as the simultaneity problem in its tendency to excess in either direction. It does, however, affect respective currency values in a floating world and can thus distort domestic policy effects. Governments and monetary authorities have to compensate. The price to be paid for the end of simultaneity could be further exchange rate instability and its consequences.

Related to the phasing question is the effect of a shift in exchange rate trends. Although the D-Mark has for 20 years been in a secular trend of strength against the dollar, the dollar may strengthen, at least for some time, if the United States pursues more restrictive monetary policies or in response to German balance of payments deficits. This might disturb the Germans because it would weaken the D-Mark and stimulate inflation in Germany, even though the Germans would welcome firming of the dollar since it would reduce the likelihood of a greater D-Mark reserve role. While the Germans do not want the dollar to be too weak, they also do not want it to be too strong—at least at the expense of the D-Mark. The Germans may sell dollars or engage in a cycle of competitive interest rate increases with the United States to protect their currency. The United States and Germany might then again be in phase, but on the downward side, complicating the problem of resuming growth for both countries. The Germans may find that they have to counteract the consequences of the very policies that they urged upon the United States. It is a difficult dilemma with no easy solution.

In a broader sense, the position of the German economy as part of the general economy of the industrial nations remains to be determined. It is clear by now that the Germans play a key role. They participate with growing confidence and growing power in the economic summits. They have shown, over the past few years, that they can set their own course even if that course takes them in a direction different from that of the United States as well as of other countries. They have even demonstrated that they can set the tone of world monetary relations by declining to go the same way as other countries. The strength of the German economy, and the strength of German currency, cannot be ignored by any senior political or economic figure in any western industrialized nation or, for that matter, even in any communist or Third World state that wishes to trade with the West.

Germany needs to find a way to become a source of stability instead of an island of stability. It will not help Germany over the long run to pursue policies that make the D-Mark stronger than other currencies, that make Germany more competitive in world trade, or that keep pyramiding German reserves, if other countries suffer the consequences of those policies. This applies not only in German relations with the United States, but also in German relations with its European Community partners. For example, any strong run from dollars into D-Marks could shatter the European Monetary System (EMS), carefully constructed by Schmidt and by French President Giscard d'Estaing as well as by several other European nations to preserve their currencies and EC trading ties against instability in the international financial system. Too many purchases of D-Marks to protect holders against weakening of the dollar would drive the D-Mark up not only against the dollar but also against other EMS currencies.

The dilemma becomes particularly acute because, while the German economy is strong enough to permit German authorities to set their own course and to influence decisions of others, it is not large enough or strong enough to substitute for the leadership role of the United States. The German economy still remains only about one third as big as the American. It is a weak instrument on which to found a world currency. German capital markets are not as large as the New York or even the London or Zurich capital markets, though this limitation is not as significant as it would have been some years ago. The German export orientation means that the Germans, far more than the Americans, need constantly to watch the effects of their policies on their international competitive position. Even as the German economy and currency have strengthened during the last few years, many Germans have been investing in America to take advantage of cheap dollars, of American growth potential, and of America's strategic security.

The German D-Mark and the U.S. dollar need the most careful coordination. Since Germany cannot become the dominant commercial and financial nation of the world within the foreseeable future, it needs consistently to think not only of influencing the policies of the United States but of coordinating with them. When, as at the end of 1979, the domestic requirements of both countries parallel each other, this appears easy. On other occasions, if the domestic requirements of the two countries do not parallel each other, it would be more difficult. Already, the Germans are concerned about the tens of billions of D-Marks that have flowed in and out of the *Bundesbank* during the last two years in response to stability problems of the dollar. A nation with the heavy export orientation of the Federal Republic cannot afford uncertainty about the secular or even the cyclical direction of its currency.

The deflationary bias of the German economy, as perceived by Americans, also raises serious questions in American eyes about the degree to which growing German dominance of the international monetary system would be disadvantageous to that system, to other countries, or even to Germany itself. This is certainly no reason to advance the theory that the recent inflationary bias of the American economy has advanced international economic stability. However, the introduction into world affairs of an important deflationary bias could, within the long run, also produce negative consequences. To the degree to which such policies begin to dominate the international system, they could create problems for that system and for the prosperity of the industrialized world. The Germans, of course, believe that they have a stability bias, not a deflationary bias, and would regard such an influence as healthy, but this would not be the American view. Disputes about macroeconomic policy under those circumstances might not be reconcilable by currency fluctuations.

The Germans cannot resolve these dilemmas by a European orientation or by closer cooperation within the European Community. Other European nations do not always follow the same economic policies as the Germans. Some have different structural problems and political attitudes from the Germans. Many Europeans disagree with German economic policies.

This said, it remains a basic truth that German and American economic interests remain similar. Germans, like Americans and many other industrialized trading nations, favor a liberal world environment. The Germans have exercised their influence within the EC to help move the EC further in the direction of a liberal world trading system. Despite the differences in German and American economic and monetary policies, the Germans have proven more than ready to collaborate with the United States in order to overcome the problems caused by those differences, where necessary. What they have not proven ready to do is to shift their basic policies to avoid differences. Neither, of course, has the United States. Therefore, coordination of policies has more often meant common management of the mechanics of the system than change in fundamental philosophies or in policies. So far, this common management has met the interests of the United States and the Federal Republic in international economic affairs.

An important element in German-American relations remains the tie between economic and political or strategic issues. The Germans have used their economic power to support their broad national interests. For example, they use trade and credits to strengthen their influence in Eastern Europe and their relations with the USSR and the GDR. They have also used it to gain political influence in the Third

World. On the other hand, Germany is vulnerable to pressures from the Organization of Petroleum Exporting Countries (OPEC). It is also subject to some jealousy from its strategic partners in NATO. German prosperity had led other Western nations, including the United States, to think the Germans should make a greater contribution to military burdens. This was one of the foundations of the offset arrangement. Pressures of that kind will not go away.

The countries of the Western World are now economically interdependent to a degree unprecedented in history. None dominates the others, yet none can escape the consequences of the others' policies, whether directly or—via the exchange market mechanism—indirectly. This makes cooperation more essential than it has ever been. At a time when the rapid growth era of the 1950s and even 1960s clearly lies behind us, the temptation to avoid coordination in order to seek one's particular salvation must be great. This can particularly affect trade relations, with protectionism felt more strongly in all the countries of the Western World. Economic and political leaders in all these nations recognize that they cannot solve their problems individually. The dilemma for them all, and particularly for the Americans and the Germans, is to reconcile these contradictions, working with other countries without sacrificing domestic imperatives or abandoning long-held economic philosophy and policy.

German and American economic power has led to considerable collaboration between the two countries and yet, on occasion, because of the different biases built into the economic systems of the two countries, has become a source of tension. German and American policy-makers have to find ways to control that tension, since it probably cannot be eliminated, and to work together to help direct the international economic system in a manner that permits both countries to thrive and to collaborate as openly and freely as in the past.

V. CONSISTENT STEWARDSHIP

After observing the greater balance in American and German power, reviewing the international environment,
and citing the psychological and historical dimensions, this
paper then examined some specifics of the formidable common agenda facing German and American policy-makers.
Discussion and examination of each problem area revealed
distinctions, sometimes subtle and sometimes not so subtle,
in German and American perceptions and situations, as well
as a potential for friction arising out of those perceptions and
out of baffling complexities of the issues themselves.

These difficulties should not be underestimated. Different
German and American situations and attitudes, or contrasting
economic experiences and philosophies, are not fleeting
phenomena that will vanish and leave transcending unanimity
in their place. They are genuine. They represent objective
problems, and they are better understood than ignored.

Nor should the destabilizing potential of the international
environment be underestimated. The likelihood of crises on
the periphery of the Eurasian continent, and even within it,
has deepened over the past decade. Such crises, with their
potential impact on the foundations of the current international system and of the Western alliance, whether in terms
of potential military confrontations, sudden energy shortages, or financial disclocations, can quickly shake established
structures and relationships when separate national establishments urgently search for haven.

In looking at these phenomena, actual and potential, one needs to look again at the German-American relationship in historical terms and ask whether it was only a hallmark of the Cold War, a spastic response to a particular threat, a temporary solution that served a vital function but that, having been re-evaluated in the light of shifting circumstances, came to seem less essential or less useful than before. History abounds with such relationships.

The question can perhaps be best answered by another question: Would the United States and the Federal Republic be better able now than in past decades to deal with potential difficulties if they were freed of their mutual ties and were to act separately? The answer is so obvious as almost to make the question appear rhetorical. Even where perceptions differ, neither country can do better by itself than it can in association with the other. There may be some tactical advantage on occasion in acting separately, but no lasting benefit. The fundamental need for stability of both countries, as well as of their neighbors, is better served when they cooperate.

The importance of cooperation emerges even more clearly when one looks at the common interests of the two countries in the specific areas reviewed by the paper. Germany and America have a common interest in maintaining a coordinated policy toward the Soviet Union. Germany and America have a common interest in a durable international political and economic environment that can weather any potential shocks. They also have a common interest in strong Western associations and in demonstrating that those associations can act decisively even in the new tedious world environment.

Historically, therefore, the German-American link could perhaps be seen not as a passing phenomenon but as part of the healing of the West after its internescine battles, and as part of an historical consolidation under the pressure of potentially destabilizing external events and forces. How far this will go remains to be seen, but one cannot dismiss out of hand that this is the process in which America and Germany are now engaged.

Multiple common interests and benefits that both countries can derive from a continuation of close relations still do not provide solutions in themselves to all the difficulties facing their association. They do, however, provide important incentives for collaboration.

In the light of those common interests, the relationship needs to be examined to see if the two countries can really collaborate to cope with the difficulties that they face. Will they be able to pursue common policies in the new world environment and under the conditions of equivalence?

In the dynamics of the German-American association, some specific factors complicate the mechanics of German-American collaboration:

—The psyschology of the relationship is troublesome. As shown in Chapter I, Americans found it easier to deal with Germans in the 1940s, 1950s, and even 1960s, when German dependence was more real and obvious than now. At present, in the wake of America's own setbacks, Americans are not always ready to accept the notion that they must deal on a basis of greater equality with a country to which the United States offers protection and for whose borders Americans are committed to lay down their lives. By the same token, on the German side, the rise toward equivalence with the United States has resulted in a tendency to deal with Americans more assertively than before, and sometimes more assertively than necessary, as if to compensate for the decades when the Germans felt materially and otherwise dependent. Young Germans also feel no personal guilt about Nazism, although they condemn it and its crimes in sharp terms, yet many Americans are very conscious of the German Nazi past. For psychological as well as historical reasons, therefore it is not always easy for Americans and Germans to deal with each other.

—Related to this is the simple reality that both Germans and Americans are tough and able, committed to success and accustomed to having their own way. Yet, in German-

American relations, neither country can have its own way most of the time. Many questions need to be settled on the basis of accommodation. That is easy to understand intellectually, less easy to accept as it is happening.

—Both countries, and Germany in particular, mourn what has been termed the "generation gap." The personalities who were, in Dean Acheson's phrase, "present at the creation," who shaped American and German foreign policy after World War II and who framed the German-American alliance within the Atlantic structure, have largely passed from the scene. Rising to take their places are others who are not as familiar with the specific problems or the particular character of the relationship. On the American side, they are not sensitive to the sober choices that Germans made when they joined NATO. On the German side, they are not conscious of the help that Americans gave to Germany in the immediate postwar years. More important, they often do not understand the central role that alliance and European structures play in the relationship and in the achievement of common German and American interests. The passing of that particular link, of senior figures who understood the basics and the context of German-American relations, and who were determined to give them a high place in Washington and Bonn policy considerations, remains a significant problem in managing the future relationship.

—The domestic dynamics in both countries with respect to the other are less favorable than before. German and American political campaigns now coincide. Ever since 1972, when a German election had to be advanced by a year, the United States and the Federal Republic have operated on the same electoral calendar. Both countries must at the same time base almost all their major decisions, and thus a significant element of their mutual relationship, upon the immediate need to fight an election campaign. Moreover, in both countries, the domestic burden of being against the other is less grave than it used to be. This applies particularly in Germany, where it is now much less costly than it used to be to take a stand known to be contrary to American views, although it has not come to the point where, as in some other countries, it is an advantage to be anti-American.

—After an election, if a new government comes to power in either country, other complications arise. New governments stress new ideas, goals, and purposes. Old governments stress established relationships. Whenever there is a change of government in either capital, Washington and Bonn can be out of phase with each other for at least some time until they recognize that new ideas may not be incompatible with old ties.

—Both countries also suffer from a general indisposition to learn very much about each other. What they do learn tends to emphasize the negative elements of each other's history. German studies in American universities do not play a role comparable to Russian studies, Chinese studies, or Japanese studies. Most American books about Germany deal not with great depth of German history and culture, but specifically with the Nazi period. On the other side, American studies lag on German campuses. Far fewer Germans than in postwar years come to America to study. Most German books about the United States focus on American problems of the last 15 years. It is as if both countries had chosen deliberately to view each other in the worst possible light. The United States appears to ignore 30 years of democracy in the Federal Republic to concentrate on 12 years of totalitarianism in the Third Reich. Germany appears to ignore 200 years of creativity and progress in America to concentrate on a time of unprecedented difficulty.

—Although bilateral and multilateral collaboration in the alliance mechanism is good, new problems erupting suddenly can confront Bonn and Washington, as well as other alliance members, without adequate coordinating mechanisms. At that point, there is a tendency to turn to crisis management techniques which often, in the first instance, ignore allies. In the modern world environment, where sudden emergencies are bound to happen, this tendency may produce a great deal of alliance and German-American friction before the Western partners settle down to collaborate. The single area in which this has been the greatest problem has been Middle East and related energy policy.

—Alliance finger-pointing about inadequate partnership contributions, hitherto largely confined to disputes about respective military contributions, has been moving into other topics, most notably energy. The Germans, along with other Europeans, have openly and repeatedly criticized American energy consumption and have asserted that the United States should permit its domestic fuel price to rise to world levels or find some other device to reduce consumption. There have also been mutual recriminations about protectionism, likely to increase when world economic conditions tighten. These attitudes detract from a cooperative spirit in the relationship as a whole.

If these factors complicate management of relations, there are others that more than compensate. Most young Germans speak English astonishingly well, far better than Americans speak German. Even if Germans no longer view the United States with the admiration and gratitude of the postwar years, they have developed within themselves a habit of dealing with American culture and an understanding of things American that far exceeds what they had in the postwar years.

Trans-national contacts are good. Trade proceeds at high levels. German investment in the United States is growing. Young businessmen, young managers, and young intellectuals travel back and forth at a high rate. There may be less contact at the senior Establishment level, but there is much greater frequency of contact at the junior level. Although not as many young Germans as during the postwar years regard it as the dream of their lives to come to America, more Germans than ever are visiting the United States as the

D-Mark has become stronger and as America has tried to attract foreign tourism.

There is also a genuine commonality of values between Americans and Germans. Both value their democratic institutions and their free way of life. The Germans, who deal more with Eastern Europeans and Russians than Americans do, are acutely conscious of the disparities between their system and the Eastern European system. They have absolutely no desire to change. The frequent trips that West Germans take to East Germany have probably done much, even while drawing Germany into closer contacts with the East, to make West Germans appreciate that their system should stay as it is.

Those who have toiled in the diplomatic vineyards also can attest to the vast range of mutual consultation and exchange of information that exists between the two countries. An astonishing number of issues, relating to the most diverse areas and problems of world affairs, are discussed virtually on a daily basis between the United States and the Federal Republic. These discussions not only cover such well-known current topics as East-West matters and energy, but the whole broad scope of political, economic, and strategic issues as well. In these discussions, difficulties and differences may and indeed do appear. What is significant, however, is that the discussions take place on a continuing basis and, for the most part, at a level of informality and good will that is rare even in alliance exchanges. They also take place against the common understanding that problems can and must be solved, against an expectation that agreement must and will come.

German-American relations suffer, in fact, from a peculiar hazard: they must not appear to become *too* good, and must under no circumatances become exclusive. Both countries worry about the establishment, or any suggestion of the establishment, of a "Bonn-Washington Axis," a particularly good German-American relationship that would dominate and thus undermine the Atlantic Community. They need to make sure that other allies not only get, but also perceive, full opportunity to collaborate with both Germany and America.

Germans clearly want the United States to maintain a position of international preeminence. Even if they disagree with American policy, they do not under any circumstances wish the United States to fall from the senior leadership role within the alliance, in East-West or in world affairs. The principal German policy solution in many questions must be to try to influence American policy, not to undermine it.

By the same token, the United States has not regarded the German rise to world power and influence as a challenge to the American position. If anything, Americans have welcomed the rising influence of the new Germany, seeing in it a vindication of American faith in the German people even after the Nazi experience. Americans also believe that German power and influence will reinforce America's position and help the Western Alliance as a whole. This has been proven correct. Even in areas where there is philosophic difference, as in the economic area, there has been very close coordination of German and American policies and the two countries have supported each other.

The relationship between the Federal Republic and the United States has become so symbiotic that neither can injure the other without injuring itself. The principal tension between them very often consists not of competing with each other, but of influencing the other to do what each wishes. Americans often speak of greater German "responsibility" in the management of world affairs, a phrase that usually means that the Americans wish the Germans to use their influence in the pursuit of policies favored by the United States, or at least to help America carry its burdens. By the same token, Germans will speak about America "accepting its responsibilities as a world leader," which often means that the United States should pursue the kinds of policies that would be advantageous to German interests, or would at least not place more weight on Germany's shoulders than the Germans want at this time. Significantly, each sees the power of the other as a potential instrument of support.

Germany wants U.S. leadership in certain directions. The United States wants German involvement, also in certain directions. The problems in the relationship arise not over American or German purposes, directions, or roles, but over the directions in which each is to use its influence. American and German complaints about each other, when they are uttered, reflect disappointments, disagreements, and irritations, not a search for alternatives. The Germans, like the Americans, can have no illusions about whether they can find others who can be equally valuable allies.

Because of these diverse considerations, the German-American association poses intricate problems of management for both sides. It would be tempting to propose that difficulties and differences be settled in a spectacular diplomatic manner, in one meeting or a series of meetings at appropriate levels, at which all problems might be discussed sequentially and resolved and laid to rest. However, while such a meeting or meetings could contribute to mutual understanding, all the problems of the relationship could not be handled in such a forum for the following reasons:

—Too many issues need to be discussed. German and American interests and issues cover virtually the entire spectrum of world affairs. Perhaps a few urgent topics could and should be addressed, but not all could or should be so handled.

—Different issues are moving at different speeds and in different frames of references. They do not all culminate at any given point in time or space. They do not conveniently array themselves for simultaneous resolution.

—Most German-American issues have a strong, and even dominant, multilateral character. Security issues have to be handled in a NATO context. Economic and/or energy issues have to be handled through such international forums as the EC, the OECD, the International Energy Agency, or the

International Monetary Fund. Other allies have a keen interest in East-West developments in East-West relations. Such multilateral considerations do not obviate the need for close coordination and consultation between Washington and Bonn, but they show that the two capitals cannot solve all problems between themselves.

Therefore, the prime instrument for German-American collaboration must be sustained and consistent handling of the difficulties as they arise or as they are perceived. There has to be a persistent stewardship, at all times and at all levels, of the links forged between the two countries in the postwar years. That stewardship must be accomplished not only by the political or diplomatic establishments, but also by the legislative, the financial, the intellectual, the military, as well as others. It cannot be handled only by the central governments, but must be pursued in the myriad contacts that exist among organizations and citizens at all levels of the relationship.

Even this kind of sustained effort does not guarantee resolution of all issues. There may be some problems that cannot be immediately solved or even handled, where specific policy interests may take precedence over considerations of the German-American association. In such cases, care can be taken that those problems that are beyond immediate solution do not poison or jeopardize the relationship as a whole. Too much is at stake, for both peoples, to proceed without due regard for the potentially adverse consequences across the whole range of the German-American association.

By the same token, neither country can afford to slide into disputes with the other by oversight or irritation. Genuine differences will be unavoidable, but there is no need or reason to create unnecessary difficulties. This is part of the task of management and stewardship.

The central realities of the relationship, however, are not the differences between the partners or the complexities of the tasks with which they have to deal. The central realities are the common direction in which both partners need to go and their respective inability to get there without the other. These determine the closeness and the value of the relationship.

Greater parity between the partners need not impede relations and should even strengthen them. Equivalence may generate certain problems, in part because it has come so swiftly that attitudes on both sides are still catching up with it, but over the long run it should provide a firmer foundation for relations than the imbalance that prevailed before. That kind of relationship could not last. It was part of an order of things that no longer exists. The new relationship can last. It represents a part of the new international environment. Equivalence has many advantages once it is recognized as a reality, since each of the partners can make valuable contributions.

The two countries do not need to stand in fascinated impotence as they and the Western system are overwhelmed by the perplexities of the twentieth and twenty-first centuries. Even if the management of German-American ties proves more exacting during the next three decades than it was during the past three decades—because of equivalence or because of the international environment—no objective factors prevent collaboration and mutual support. With sustained and persistent effort on both sides, an open and intimate relationship should continue, constituting a vital element in the security and well-being of both nations.

References

American Academy of Arts and Sciences (1979) Looking for Europe. Daedalus. Vol. 108, No. 1.

ARON, R. (1979) "From Yankee imperialism to Soviet hegemony?" Encounter (August).

AZRAEL, J., LOEWENTHAL, R. and NAKAGAWA, T. (1978) An Overview of East-West Relations. New York, Tokyo and Paris: The Trilateral Commission.

BARK, D. (1974) Agreement on Berlin. A study of the 1970-72 Quadripartite Negotiations. Stanford: Hoover Institution.

BERGSTEN, C. (1975) "The United States and Germany." Bergsten. Toward a New International Economic Order. Lexington: Heath.

––– (1975) The Dilemmas of the Dollar. New York: New York University Press.

BURNS, A. (1978) The Dollar and the International Monetary System. Washington: American Enterprise Institute.

CALLAGHAN, T. (1979) "A new North-Atlantic treaty of technological cooperation and trade." Paper presented to conference sponsored by Center for Strategic and International Studies, Georgetown University. Brussels, (September).

CALLEO, D. (1978) The German Problem Reconsidered. Cambridge: Cambridge University Press.

CATUDAL, H. (1978) A Balance Sheet of the Quadripartite Agreement on Berlin. Berlin: Berlin Verlag.

CLINE, R. (1980) World Power Trends and U.S. Foreign Policy for the 1980s. Boulder: Westview.

CROAN, M. (1976) East Germany: The Soviet Connection. The Washington Papers, No. 36.

DAVIS, J. and PFALTZGRAFF, R. (1978) Soviet Theater Strategy: Implications for NATO. Washington: United States Strategic Institute.

DE MAIZIERE, U. (1976) Armed Forces in the NATO Alliance. Center for Strategic and International Studies, Georgetown University.

DE PORTE, A. (1979) Europe Between the Super-Powers. New Haven: Yale University Press.

DETTKE, D. (1976) Allianz im Wandel. Frankfurt: Metzner.

DILL, M. (1961) Germany: A Modern History. Ann Arbor: University of Michigan Press.

DOENHOFF, M. (1979) "Bonn and Washington: the strained relationship." Foreign Affairs, Vol. 57, No. 5.

DUNN, L. (1979) "Half past India's bang." Foreign Policy, No. 36.

ERMARTH, F. (1978) "Contrasts in American and Soviet Strategic Thought." International Security, Vol. 3, No. 2.

Federal Minister of Defense (1979) The Security of the Federal Republic of Germany and the Development of the Federal Armed Forces. White Paper. Bonn.

Federal Republic of Germany (1977). Texts Relating to the European Political Co-operation. Bonn.

FELLNER, W., Project Director. (1979) Contemporary Economic Problems. Washington: American Enterprise Institute.

GASTEYGER, K. (1976) Die Beiden Deuschen Staaten in der Weltpolitik. Munich: Piper.

GESSERT, R. and SEIM, H. (1977) "Improving NATO's Theater Nuclear Posture: A Reassessment and a Proposal." Center for Strategic and International Studies, Georgetown University.

GORDON, R. and PELKMANS, M. (1979) Challenges to Interdependent Economies. 1980s Project/Council on Foreign Relations. New York: McGraw-Hill.

GREENWOOD, T., et al. (1977) Nuclear Power and Weapons Proliferation. Adelphi Papers No. 130. London: International Institute for Strategic Studies.

GRIFFITH, W. (1979) "The West German-American relationship." Washington Quarterly, Vol. 2, No. 3.

HABERLER, G. (1978) The State of the World Economy and the International Monetary System. Washington: American Enterprise Institute.

HAHN, W. and PFALTZGRAFF, L. (eds.) (1979) Atlantic Community In Crisis. New York: Pergamon Press.

HASSNER, P. (1979) "Intra-Alliance diversities and challenges: NATO in an age of hot peace." Paper presented to conference sponsored by Center for Strategic and International Studies, Georgetown University. Brussels (September 1979).

HILLENBRAND, M. (1977) "NATO and Western Security in an Era of Transition." International Security, Vol. 2, No. 2.

HOFFMANN, S. (1979) "New variations on old themes." International Security, Vol. 4, No. 1.

HOLBORN, H. (1969) A History of Modern Germany, 1840-1945. New York: Knopf.

HUNTINGTON, S. (1979) "American foreign policy: the changing political universe." The Washington Quarterly, Vol. 2, No. 4.

International Institute for Strategic Studies (1978) The Military Balance 1978-79. Dorking: Bartholomew Press.

––– (1979) The Military Balance 1979-80. Dorking: Bartholomew Press.

International Monetary Fund (1979) International Financial Statistics. Washington, D.C. (December).

JORDAN, A., et al. (1979) Facing the International Energy Problem. New York: Praeger.

KAISER, K. (1968) German Foreign Policy in Transition. London and New York: Oxford.

——— (1978) "The great nuclear debate: German-American Disagreements." Foreign Policy, No. 30.

——— and SCHWARZ, H. (eds.) (1977) America and Western Europe: Problems and Prospects. Lexington: Heath.

KATZENSTEIN, P. (ed.) (1978) Between Power and Plenty. Madison: University of Wisconsin Press.

KELLEHER, C. (1975) Germany and the Politics of Nuclear Weapons. New York and London: Columbia University Press.

KISSINGER, H. (1979) "The Future of NATO." The Washington Quarterly, Vol. 2, No. 4.

——— (1979) White House Years. Boston: Little Brown.

KLETT, R. and POHL, W. (1979) Stationen Einer Republik. Stuttgart: DVA.

KNAPP, M. et al. (1978) Die USA and Deutschland, 1918-1975. Munich: Beck.

KNAPP, M. (1979) "Das Deutsch-Amerikanische Verhaeltnis im Spannungsfeld zwischen Politik und Wirtschaft." Amerikastudien, Vol. 24, No. 1.

KOMER, R. (1979) "Looking Ahead." International Security, Vol. 4, No. 1.

LAQUEUR, W. (1979) A Continent Astray: Europe 1970-78. Oxford: Oxford University Press.

LIVINGSTON, R. (1976) "Germany steps up." Foreign Policy, No. 22.

LOEWENTHAL, R. (1978) "Why German stability is so insecure." Encounter, Vol. LI, No. 6.

MAHNCKE, D. (1972) Nukleare Mitwirkung. Berlin: De Gruyter.

MAKINS, C. (1979) "Negotiating European security: The next steps." Survival, Vol. XXL, No. 6.

METZGER, R. and DOTY, P. (1978/79) "Arms control enters the gray area." International Security, Vol. 3, No. 3.

MOODIE, M. (1979) "Sovereignty, Security, and Arms." The Washington Papers, No. 67.

MORGAN, R. (1974) The United States and West Germany, 1945-1973. Oxford: Oxford University Press.

——— (1978) West Germany's Foreign Policy Agenda. The Washington Papers, No. 54.

MYERS, K. (1972) Ostpolitik and American Security Interests in Europe. Center for Strategic and International Studies, Georgetown University.

NERLICH, U. (1975/76) Nuclear Weapons and East-West Negotiation. Adelphi Papers, No. 120. London: International Institute for Strategic Studies.

——— (1978) Die Verbesserung der nuklearen Faehigkeiten der NATO. Ebenhausen: Stiftung Wissenschaft und Politik.

NUNN, S. and BENNETT, C. (1977) Allied Partnership in Armaments, Trans-Atlantic Seminar. Center for Strategic and International Studies, Georgetown University.

NYE, J. (1978) "Non-Proliferation." Foreign Affairs, Vol. 56, No. 3.

OSGOOD, R. (1968) Alliances and American Foreign Policy. Baltimore and London: Johns Hopkins.

Second German-American Roundtable on NATO: The Theater Nuclear Balance. Summary of a Transatlantic Dialogue. (1978) Konrad-Adenauer-Stiftung and Institute for Foreign Policy Analysis. Cambridge, Mass.

88

TEW, B. (1977) The Evolution of the International Monetary System 1945-77. London: Hutchinson.

TREVERTON, G. (1978) The Dollar Drain and American Forces in Germany. Athens: Ohio University Press.

——— (1979) "Nuclear weapons and the 'Gray Area'." Foreign Affairs, Vol. 57, No. 5.

U.S. Congress, House (1979) Committee on Armed Services. Report of Special Subcommittee on NATO Standardization, Interoperability and Readiness. 95th Congress, 2d session. Washington: Government Printing Office.

U.S. Congress, Senate (1979) Committee on Foreign Relations. A Staff Report to the Subcommittee on European Affairs. SALT and the NATO Allies. 96th Congress, 1st session. Washington: Government Printing Office.

U.S. Congress (1979) Joint Economic Committee. A Compendium of Papers submitted to the Joint Economic Committee. The U.S. Role in a Changing World Political Economy: Major Issues for the 96th Congress. 1st session. Washington: Government Printing Office.

U.S. Department of Defense Annual Report (1980).

VARDIMIS, A. (1979) "German-American military fissures." Foreign Policy, No. 34.

WETTIG, G. (1976) Die Sowjetunion, die DDR und die Deutschland-Frage, 1965-1976. Stuttgart: Bonn Aktuell.